Second Cup
Collected Columns

Mary Adams Belk

Solomon & George Publishers
301 Lee Road 15
Auburn, AL 36830

1. Non-fiction

ISBN: 978-0-9853404-4-5

First Edition

10 9 8 7 6 5 4 3 2 1

Table of Contents

Worldly Goods

On the Road

Back in the Day

Happy Holidays

Pondering

Introduction by Joe McAdory

She can take you somewhere you've never been, and make you feel right at home.

She can tell you about a person you've never met, and make them feel like family.

She will take you back to the era of innocence, and make you appreciate where you came from.

She will tell you about mishaps and missteps, misfits and mistakes, and at the same time bring out the hero in everybody.

Mary Belk is pure, small-town, Southern Americana. She writes from the sleeve. She writes from the heart.

She is conversational, witty, and compelling.

Mary brings the heart of old Auburn, Alabama—spoiled today by corporate commercialism and national chain stores—back to life. She takes us inside those old mom 'n pop family-owned thrift shops, when Glenn-Dean Drugs was actually a store and not an intersection, and inside the beloved and cozy Kopper Kettle Diner, where locals shared breakfast (and gossip) together on Alabama mornings. The Kopper Kettle was tragically, and without injury, blown to smithereens early one 1978 morning. God bless Mary for bringing its morning coffee and toast back to our breakfast tables.

Today's modern conveniences have replaced yesterday's charm, just like interstate highways have taken many travelers off the two-lane thoroughfares that, more times than not, enrich our journeys. Sometimes it's good to stop and smell the roses. Mary does just that through the written word, whether it's a simple road trip with the family or the journey of life that carried her from the banks of the Chattahoochee River and West Point, Georgia, as a young child, to Virginia, and finally home to the Loveliest Village on the Plain.

But there's more to Mary than reminiscing about nostalgia. She's funny. Reading Mary, we learn of her great affection for spring cleaning (sarcasm), a great desire to light the fireplace at Christmastime even if it is 80 degrees outside, and her humorous attitude about growing old. According to Mary, "You know you're getting old when 'People who are 30-something call you ma'am' and 'The doctor comes in and you think it's his teen-age son.'"

Mary has the ability to create humor from an otherwise negative situation. Life hands us difficult challenges every day. We can choose to reject them and find fault in anything other than ourselves, or accept them, learn from them, and, in some cases, turn our own misfortune into laughter. Mary does this, and does it well.

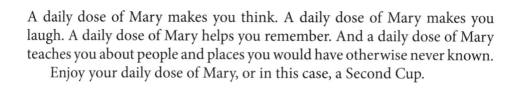

A daily dose of Mary makes you think. A daily dose of Mary makes you laugh. A daily dose of Mary helps you remember. And a daily dose of Mary teaches you about people and places you would have otherwise never known.

Enjoy your daily dose of Mary, or in this case, a Second Cup.

Joe McAdory is former columnist and Editorial Page Editor for the *Opelika-Auburn News*. He is now Communications Editor for the Auburn University Raymond J. Harbert College of Business.

Family, Friends, and Heroes

"I am part of all I have met."

Alfred, Lord Tennyson

Celestine Sibley

The story didn't make the local daily news the other morning and most television stations didn't bother with it. But *The Atlanta Constitution* announced front-page center: "She wrote her name on a region: The South mourns Celestine Sibley."

Sibley, whose column ran in the *Constitution* for 55 years, died at the age of 85. She was "one of the South's natural wonders," author Pat Conroy said. Best known for her folksy homespun columns she wrote about everything from gardens to politics, her family and Southern traditions. Whatever Sibley wrote, it seems she touched a chord with readers.

"Ceslestine Sibley reminds us of the endless pleasures of our ordinary lives," former Georgia Governor Zell Miller once said. "She refocuses our attention on what really matters—family, friends, the wonder of the changing seasons and the view from our back yards."

Sibley was raised in the piney woods country north of Mobile. At Murphy High she was editor of the school paper. And at 15 she got her first newspaper job with the *Mobile Press*. In 1941 she moved to Atlanta and was told by *The Atlanta Journal's* city editor that he didn't like women reporters because they distracted the men in the newsroom. So she took a job at the *Constitution* for $35 a week.

"I covered every beat in town… and gradually became a regular at murder trial coverage," she wrote in her memoir. "There were others who could do it as well, but none enjoyed a good trial as much as I did."

Sibley viewed capital trials as the modern-day counterpart to Shakespeare's theater. Her fictional alter ego, Katherine Kincaid, the newswriting protagonist in her first novel, *The Malignant Heart*, summed it up, "Murder is my favorite assignment."

When editor Ralph McGill asked Sibley to write a column for the *Constitution* in 1945, she told him she had nothing to write about. Then she mentioned that her three children were having problems with their tonsils, and he suggested she write about that. She did. And her down-home column became a favorite with loyal readers who thought of Sibley as a good friend. Her warm, simple writing style drew them into her thoughts and her life as she told about washing and ironing curtains, digging in the garden, and enjoying spring and summer vegetables.

In 1958, Sibley started covering politics and the Legislature. She covered that beat for 20 years. And she was adept at coaxing quotes from career politicians. Georgia Governor Roy Barnes said, "Celestine knew the secrets on all of us in the General Assembly, and we were comfortable that she knew."

In 1998 she had heart trouble and underwent angioplasty. Four days later she stubbornly went back to work writing about the adventure. In her typical droll style she wrote: "So one night, lacking anything better to do, I had a heart attack."

She had undergone surgery for breast cancer in 1995. Late last year she learned that the cancer had returned. But she kept on writing, and those last columns sometimes dealt with heaven, sleepless nights, and having to give up driving.

Sibley captured the language, the rhythm, and the flavor of the Deep South in more than 10,000 columns for *The Atlanta Constitution*, countless news stories and 25 books.

Celestine Sibley, the prodigious chronicler of a half-century of Southern life is gone. Through her columns we saw the South she loved. We felt we knew her. And we mourn her loss.

Charlie Rose

What does an English professor, retired after 34 years, do with the rest of his life? Anything he wants to you might say. But this isn't a riddle, and it's not a rhetorical question. I'm referring to Charles Rose and his memoir *In the Midst of Life*.

Close your eyes and conjure up a hot September day in 1997. This is when it all started as Rose hunkered in the back of Burger King scanning the Community Calendar in the *Auburn Bulletin*. There were organizations needing volunteers—Project Uplift and the local literacy outreach program. Good groups, but not for him. Then he noticed Hospice volunteers were in demand. Maybe, he thought, just maybe.

Although he felt the tug, he kept wondering why he needed to do Hospice. Then one afternoon while navigating the back roads of Lee County, rattling over bridges, passing waterfalls and sheep-pocked hills, he got stuck behind a log truck. As he sat pondering what he was considering doing, scattered memories of dying relatives came to him and the thought of becoming a hospice volunteer took on renewed meaning.

So Charles Rose sat with terminally ill patients, visiting with them and looking into their lives. When his wife suggested that he write down his thoughts, he started a journal, jotting down their memories, precisely recording their condition, details about their health. He took notes and drew pictures, reported his impressions and feelings describing his two year experience in the late nineties as a hospice volunteer. His memories were crammed with images, sounds, smells, recollections of places and people's faces and odd remarks made in passing. He reflected on what it all meant.

Finally it was time for him to plant himself in a chair and tell the story he'd found out. Some writers choose fiction as an approach to truth. Rose chose a memoir, a reflection of his late-life, post-retirement experience. Seems that more compelling than fictional misery is real life suffering.

As a volunteer, Rose had the option of choosing what he wanted to do when he got there. Sometimes he talked, drew sketches, or just offered his presence. His decision to read aloud to three of his four patients took me back to my childhood sick-days lying in bed with my mother sitting in a straight-back chair reading my favorite books to me.

Rose's use of literature to transport a suffering individual to a different time and place also brought to mind another memoir, Azar Nafisi's *Reading Lolita in Tehran*. The young women who gathered every Thursday in Nafisi's living room risked removing their veils and steeped themselves in the worlds of Jane Austen, F. Scott Fitzgerald, Henry James, and Vladimir Nabokov.

It told of the freeing power of literature. Like Nafisi, Rose leaves a path of sadness and loss in his sparkling memoir.

He read passages from the Bible to Lonnie Simmons, a 76-year-old black man. And for Larry Beckwith, a retired chemistry professor, he picked *The Hobbit*. In real life things tend to happen out of order, not like we'd planned. After agonizing on what to read to World War II veteran Howard Carr, he finally settled on *Huck Finn*, but when he took the dog-eared paperback novel from his pocket and opened it up, the first four chapters were missing. At first he panicked, then he gave a quick synopsis and began the story, happy to see that Carr smiled at the funny parts.

Rose became a hospice volunteer reluctantly but came away with a treatise on how life shapes the meaning of death. Using the technique of narrative fiction, Rose presents sharp portraits of his subjects without a smidgen of sentiment or sermonizing. He simply tells what he experienced.

It's books such as this that remind us why we read in the first place.

Jane

There's nothing like a sister. I had the good fortune to be blessed with three of them—just the right number to fulfill my every need. Barbara, Beth and Jane were everything in my young world.

Jane and I were closest in age. She was three-and-a-half years older, but for many years we were more like twins. Jane was my soul mate, my confidant, my playmate, my role model, my leader and my sidekick. Growing up, we were a package deal. If you asked Jane to come to your house to play or to your birthday party, her reply was always the same—"Can Mary come?" If I wasn't invited, the deal was off. We pretty much preferred to play by ourselves anyway. But usually, they wanted Jane enough to put up with me.

My mother said I didn't learn to walk—I went from crawling to running, my short legs pumping for all they were worth to keep up with my athletic sister. And when she started school, I would sit in the rocking chair looking out the window waiting for Jane to come home.

Who I became was shaped by my sister Jane. I took piano lessons for three months then quit because Jane did, and sang alto in the Methodist youth choir because she did.

We played with gusto and intensity. She was The Lone Ranger; I was Tonto. She was Jesse James; I was Frank. She was Tarzan; I was Boy. She was the pitcher; I was the catcher. She was the charmer, and I was happy to follow.

We lay in bed at night listening to our favorite programs on a small brown box of a radio—"Ozzie and Harriet," "Our Miss Brooks," Brooklyn Dodgers baseball, and of course "The Lone Ranger."

On Saturday afternoons we walked barefoot to the Tiger Theater to watch Roy Rogers, Francis the Talking Mule, and Ma and Pa Kettle. And when we got a television set, we laughed deep belly laughs watching George Gobel and the "Sid Caesar Show of Shows."

Now she's gone and I'm left shell-shocked not knowing quite who I am. Scores of friends write from all over the world saying that she'd blessed their lives. And I wonder how one small woman who spent most of her life in a college town without getting a degree made such a difference in the lives of so many. She was the embodiment of Mother Teresa's words, "Few of us can do great things, but all of us can do small things with great love."

I sat by her bed at Bethany House holding her hand. I closed my eyes, and we were children again skating lickety-split down cracked sidewalks, running breathless along the banks of the Chattahoochee River, zipping down the big slide at Felton Little Park with our dog Sambo close behind, making ink out of poke berries and camp stew out of dirt and water, propped in bed in the heat of the day reading to the drone of the oscillating fan.

Now I'm left with a hurt so deep, seems I'm a worker-bee carrying a load heavier than my own weight. I cling to the cliché that time will heal, like the little girl I used to be, looking out the window, rocking and waiting.

Old Friends

It's funny about friendship. I've wondered for years—why is it that we like some people more than others?

My friend Ruthie and I have nothing in common. There's no good reason in this world for us to have bonded in the first place much less to have kept our friendship alive and well for forty-something years.

I grew up in the Deep South, a Methodist of Scotch-Irish descent. I went to college in the turbulent '60s at conservative, WASPish Auburn University. Ruthie grew up Jewish in California. She spent her college years in that same era of unrest at liberal, ethnic San Francisco State.

We first met when we were sophomores in college, and something just clicked. I was a 19-year-old newlywed, and she was engaged to my husband's best friend from high school. Mike and Ruthie flew to Atlanta that summer, and after visiting with kinfolk, we drove them back home in our un-air-conditioned Volkswagen Beetle that was stuffed with maps, guidebooks, a Coleman lantern, and an ice chest. Our suitcases were strapped to the lopsided luggage rack up top, and there were pots and pans, tents and duffel bags tied to the front of the lime-green Bug.

We lived those days slowly and in a closeness that gave us the opportunity, as well as the leisure, for awareness of tastes, responses, habits—and foibles. We chugged down winding two-lane highways and camped at Red Rock Canyon, Oklahoma; the Grand Canyon; and Las Vegas, New Mexico. We spread ham-sandwich lunches on a quilt at the Continental Divide, the Petrified Forest and Death Valley. And somewhere along Rt. 66, after only occasional rumblings of mutiny, we came to the tacit agreement that our differences didn't matter half as much as the fact that we liked each other an awful lot.

We've kept up with each other in a disjointed kind of way. Other than a quick note now and then, we don't write, but once in a blue moon, she heads east or I go west. Whenever that happens, as soon as Ruthie and I spot each other, we start laughing and talking non-stop like teenagers at a lock-in.

Not long ago, after years of separation and silence, we met at a Florida beach. As always, Ruthie and I talked as if we'd never stopped. We came together as easily as shells wash up on the shore. With the bright sunshine piercing the Perdido Key sky, the years melted away. We dodged jellyfish in the gulf and walked barefoot in the wet sand, gathering seashells and chattering over the squawk of gulls. For a few days, I forgot that any other place existed. All that mattered was an old friend, lost years, shared memories, and the awareness of parting again too soon.

And in the end, I don't really regret that Ruthie and I have so little in common. I'm just happy that we can sustain a friendship for forty years simply because whenever we meet something clicks.

Queen Lilibet

Maybe it's the anthropologist in me, but I'm bone tired, sick to death, of Americans trying to shove middle-class, twenty-first century norms down the throat of the Queen of England. And Britons who are doing the same had best be glad it's Elizabeth II on the throne instead of Henry VIII. Remember Henry? He's the one who was akin to *Alice in Wonderland's* Queen of Hearts stamping about in a furious passion shouting, "Off with his head!" and "Off with her head!"

I doubt if many Americans know much about the British monarchy and much less about the Queen herself. The thing I keep hearing is that the Queen is boring.

Would we like the 79-year-old queen more if she fooled around behind Prince Philip's back and rode off into the sunset with, say, Sean Connery or an Arab Sheik? Maybe you would, but not me. I think she's a fascinating woman and a class act just the way she is.

Lilibet, as she's known to her family, had her first horseback riding lesson as a 2-year-old. For her third Christmas she was given her own pony and could soon ride it well.

Magazines and newspapers liked to run pictures of the princess when she was growing up. She was exotic and glamorous whether riding a horse or posing prettily in a white gown. People followed her comings and goings the way Americans followed the events in the lives of the Kennedy children.

Seems there are some trappings that accompany the glamorous life of royalty. She never went to school but had private lessons at home. And she stood during many of her lessons so she would get used to standing for long periods of time without tiring.

Princess Elizabeth turned 16 during WWII. She wanted to work as a volunteer nurse in the blitzed area of London, but her father, King George VI, thought she was too young. Three years later he let her join a wartime vehicle maintenance class. A picture of Elizabeth on her knees, clad in drab army-green coveralls and cap, changing the tire on a military truck reminds me of the famous photo of Rosy the Riveter.

The Royal Family stayed at Buckingham Palace throughout the war, even though most of the windows were totally without glass because of the bombing. And they ate strictly according to the ration book. At the end of WWII, Winston Churchill declared that King George VI and his family had more closely identified with their people in war than had any of their predecessors.

On a gray, wintry day in February of 1952 the King died. Four thousand miles away in a hunting lodge in Kenya, a telephone call conveyed the sad news to the young woman who was now, quite suddenly, Queen Elizabeth II.

Elizabeth carried out her royal duties and at the same time was the devoted "Mummy" of four children. Prince Charles was four years old before he learned from a servant that Mummy was the Queen.

With her shoes kicked off, the Sovereign Queen works at a desk that is lined with photos of children, horses, guns and dogs. On the carpet lie several small, fierce, plump Welsh Corgies.

Queen Elizabeth isn't allowed to vote. She goes shopping once a year. And she has no last name. But she does attend her favorite sport—horse racing.

The thing that always touches me about Queen Elizabeth is that whenever she makes an official statement she has those clear plastic dollar-ninety-eight glasses perched on her nose.

Some say it's time to do away with the monarchy. But I say, "God save the Queen!"

Sister Week

Today is hot and still and dry, so there's nothing much to do except stay inside and mull over matters. Past summers come to mind, and the longer I ponder, the more I think about Mama and her six sisters. There were twelve Corbitt children in all. Two died at a young age, and that left seven girls and three boys. Even though Aunt Alma was twenty when Mama, the "baby," was born, the sisters always stayed in close touch. The three nurses lived in far off places—Aunt Mary in Miami, Aunt Alma and Aunt Theresa in Charleston, West Virginia. But when it came to keeping in touch, they were inflexible. They were adamant about writing Round-Robin letters every month and getting together at Christmastime. And once a year they spent a week together, sequestered, having no contact with the outside world.

The get-togethers started at Aunt Louise's moss-green stucco house on Cherry Street in Eufaula, their native town. Then Aunt Mary moved back close to home and built a snug little house up the hill from my family's cabin in the piney-woods. After that, the gatherings took place in that secluded compound, with the sisters traipsing down the path from the cottage to the cabin and back.

Rooting through boxes of memorabilia, I found part of a *Valley-Daily Times News*. It was brownish and brittle, with a front-page article, "Sister Week Held by 7 Corbitt Sisters." The date was missing, but the picture was from the early 1950s. The article quoted Aunt Jenny, "You know, we really live the life of Riley down here for a whole week—just eating, sleeping, reading, listening to music, and talking— mostly just talking. When seven women, especially seven sisters, get together only once a year, there's plenty to talk about!"

I can replay those Sister Weeks in vivid, living color. I'm pretty sure I was the only person who ever witnessed the fun, other than the cook my daddy hired for the week so the sisters could "just loaf." Family members weren't allowed to visit until the end of the week when the Corbitt clan met for a family reunion. But when I was a slip of a girl, I'd drive up at noon, unannounced, and they would insist that I join them for dinner. Once I showed up in the late afternoon and caught the gray-haired sisters in their baggy bathing suits laughing and splashing in the 6-1/2 by 8-foot pool that Daddy had built for my sister Jane and me.

Sitting under the humming ceiling fan, I remember leaving the cabin before dark fell to drive the twenty miles home. On the seat beside me was a sweet smelling leftover morsel Aunt Ruby had wrapped in waxed paper. I felt full and much loved as I headed back to my life as a slaphappy teenager. I realize now that the sisters had stuffed me with more than a mouth watering meal. Most of all they'd fed my soul.

Teachers

"Why do you always get the interesting teachers?" my friend asked me forty-something years ago. It was the first day of fall quarter and I had just described my English lit professor to her; told her about the man in khaki pants, plaid shirt and tennis shoes. About how awesome he was in a laid back kind of way. About his subtle sense of humor and his tousled hair. And about his unusual name—Oxford Stroud. I don't remember how many cuts we were allowed, but I wouldn't have skipped his class for anything.

Turns out my friend was right. I had more than my fair share of good teachers. I took classical literature one steamy summer quarter. Ward Allen made the course so stimulating that for an hour every morning I forgot about the tropical heat. He was the epitome of the Southern gentleman standing straight-backed as a toddler in his seersucker suit, starched white dress shirt, narrow tie and wire-rimmed glasses. His voice was soft and pleasant and he interpreted Greek drama in such a way that my mouth still curves up at the thought of *Aeschylus* or *Aristophanes*.

Madison Jones, Auburn University's long-time writer-in-residence, taught me about fiction writing. He lounged behind his desk and in his deep, raspy voice read our stories aloud. When he said he actually liked mine, I mustered up the courage to start submitting short stories for publication.

But interesting teachers weren't limited to the English department. There was Fran French, the only anthropologist at Auburn in the 1960s. She taught me everything I needed to know about anthropology. And she taught me how to look at life in new ways, and that actions always have consequences. I would have signed up for advanced mongoose milking if she'd been the teacher.

Allen Shields was the criminology department in those days. His lectures were captivating because he told us about his work with prisoners. He'd puff casually on his straight-stemmed pipe and relate case studies of criminals doing time at Kilby, Draper or Tutwiler. I took every course he taught and went with him to the prisons several times.

When I became a teacher I realized they had to put up with erratic attendance, the occasional whiney student, stacks of papers to grade and long committee meeting. Sometimes I wondered if my lectures were growing stale. I'd have to delve deep for the energy to fuel my teaching, wondering—did I learn anything about teaching from my mentors?

One day I overheard a student in my class make a comment that I'll always cherish. "Why would anybody want to skip this class?" she remarked to her friend. "It's too much fun."

Comments like that are few and far between for teachers. When I was a student, it never occurred to me to tell a teacher, "Way to go!" But I can see the truth of a bumper sticker I spied recently. It said, "If you can read this, thank a teacher."

The Four Seasons

"There is a season for every
activity under the sun."

Ecclesiastes

Fall Air

"You'd better wear a jacket," my daughter hollered as I headed out the door for my nightly constitutional. "The air's chilly tonight." I'd been waiting to hear those words for a long time.

Fall always gets short-changed. I've known long, cold winters and longer hot summers. I've seen springs that linger, but it seems I'm always waiting for autumn. It just isn't fair.

Autumn never comes soon enough for me as summer drags on for an eternity. After Labor Day, I start marking days off the calendar. I realize, of course, that the first day of fall never resembles the real thing. But on that day, summer is officially over, and that's important to me.

This year, the morning of the first day of fall was hot and humid. The sun was scorching. People were still wearing cotton dresses or shorts and sandals. I sniffed the air and said, "That fall smell isn't here yet. It's still summertime."

Every season has its own smell, and the scent of autumn was still absent. But three weeks later, there was a definite nip in the air when I took my evening stroll, and I filled my nostrils with that early fall aroma.

Certain fragrances trigger memories. As surely as a photograph in a tattered scrapbook makes me remember, a single autumn smell can take me back in time. I get a lung full of autumn air, and in a heartbeat, I'm transported back to grammar school. We sit at our little desks coloring pictures of orange pumpkins and funny black pilgrim hats. Red, yellow and gold leaves. The spicy smell of crayons fills my head as I think back. Brand new supplies at the beginning of school have their own odors. The fresh smell of notebook paper. The pungent scent of the eraser at one end of a pencil, and the tangy lead-and-wood aroma at the other end.

In the fall, football was all-important in the Loveliest Village. Most women had a lemon-yellow mum to wear to the Saturday afternoon game. The mums were bigger than a bagel and had a blue pipe-cleaner AU in the middle. Coeds stood on Toomer's Corner holding cardboard boxes filled with the game-day flowers, and the dry peppery tang saturated the air.

The stadium at game time had its own odor. Shakers made of thin strips of crepe paper were so dry that when they were waved, a cloud of sour smelling dust hung over the student section. And there was the stifling scent of cigarette smoke mingled with the sweet, fermented smell of cheap bourbon. Sorority girls smelled of expensive designer perfumes, while older women wore the drugstore brands.

Sometimes the fragrance of fall will take me back to marching band practice on a field of dead grass lined with chalk. Just calling that dusty, chalky aroma to mind makes me wheeze.

If I'm driving in my car when I catch that first whiff of fall, I turn the radio to the nearest oldies station and pump up the volume. I'm nineteen again. My world doesn't contain piles of dirty laundry, leaky faucets or grocery lists. I suppose the smell of fall makes me feel that I, too, am fresh and just beginning.

The smell of fall is new-sprung. So I still have plenty to look forward to—spicy pumpkin pie and hardwood smoldering in the fireplace. It doesn't get much better than this.

Fireplace Fire

The last fireplace fire of the season should be a time of celebration—a gathering of family and friends, the breaking of bread, the sharing of stories, the singing of songs. But no matter how much the weatherman claims to know about the weather that's coming, no matter how hard I listen, how carefully I watch the sky and check the thermometer, the weather just isn't predictable.

This year's winter has been so mild there's hardly been an excuse to build a fire at all. There were a few frosty days in November and December, but we lit logs sparingly, hoarding the hardwood, saving it for thermometer-dipping nights in January and February. And, yes, we had some lovely red-hot fires. But those two-dog nights were far and few between. So now the woodpile is as straight and tall as a Nutcracker soldier, and March is half gone.

Problem is I can't figure if cold weather is over or not. Yeah, yeah, I know. The groundhog saw his shadow. But I wonder if we've already seen the last of the ice and sleet and bitter-blowing wind. And if so, did we have the last fireplace fire of the year and not know it?

We never had home fires burning when I was a little girl. My daddy grew up in the days when heating and cooking were done by the wood-stove method. He failed to see the aesthetic appeal of leaping flames racing up the chimney, and he couldn't fathom why in the world anybody would chop and split wood when there was a perfectly good heat pump attached to the house.

There have been times in my adult life when we used the fireplace for practical purposes. Times when icy rain blew in from Yankee-land and covered the electric lines layer upon layer until they snapped. With no electric heat the family hearth became our only source of warmth. We used the orange coals to boil pans of water for brewing coffee in an old drip-o-later, and roast hot dogs or toast bread on straightened coat hangers. But mainly we've built family fires for our own creature comfort. Fires to sit close to while we play Boggle or put together jigsaw puzzles. Fires to look at for pure pleasure.

I never take a single fire for granted. After everyone else has gone to bed for the night, I drag in one more log and shove it into the simmering coals. I'm not skilled at stoking fires, but I work hard, adding a bit of kindling and a wad of newspaper, prodding and pulling with the poker. Once the flames begin to jump, I scoot a soft chair close to the hearth, and armed with a cup of tea and a good book, I stay until the ashes grow cold.

Thing is, I want to make the last fire of the season an event. But I can't be sure there'll be another cold rainy night.

There's a Web site that promises a weather forecast up to a year in advance with 83 percent accuracy. So I'm supposed to be able to log on to that site and find out when the last fireplace fire of the season will be.

They swear they know. We'll see.

Hot Weather

Hot weather and ambition don't go together very well, and I'm continually amazed at the vitality children have in extreme temperatures. Seems kids just go on having fun no matter what the heat index.

Many a child who has a yard to play in also has a playground set. This is usually a concoction of chains and poles and an assortment of somewhat smaller versions of the equipment found on city playgrounds—swings, slides, seesaws, trapezes and rings.

When I was a little girl in Auburn, to have such marvels in your own backyard would've been like having just emerged victorious from the Revlon isolation booth on TV's "The $64,000 Question." If we wanted an outlet for our energy, the only play equipment we had at our North College Street doorstep was mostly contrived out of a lot of elbow grease and imagination.

For high-class pleasure I took a barefoot walk to Felton Little Park where there was a heavenly array of clanking, shining playground equipment. Uncontested king of the park was the proud and ominous slide. It stood, its lofty head in the trees, stoically gazing over the grass, the sun reflecting splendidly off its swooping curves. It was so high that little children had to be accompanied up the ladder and held on a lap going down. To impress first-time visitors, I'd go down backwards or head first or scale the steep and slippery slope on foot with my black Cocker Spaniel in hot pursuit.

This slide was usually very slick, especially after I greased it by putting a sheet of wax paper under the seat of my pants. It was so tall and its curves so smooth that I'd go lickety-split and shoot off several feet into the grass. Now and then some child would crack his noggin and have to be led away bleeding to be bandaged before another go.

Back then people didn't seem concerned about accidents. If you got hurt, your mother took a clean rag, wiped off the blood and painted on some Mercurochrome.

The broad wooden merry-go-round with chains and handholds affixed to a giant metal pole was also popular and perilous. Back and forth, round and round it went, banging into the center pole until its riders were dizzy and dazed. Standing on this spinning device four feet off the ground was way too dangerous for young children who were shooed off to the smaller traditional merry-go-round that poked up from the dirt.

Less dangerous were the chain swings. They seemed to me sky-high as I soared heavenward pumping for all I was worth. Then there would be a snap and a jerk and someone would yell, "You're gonna go over!" Kids were always claiming they had whirled over the top, but we never quite believed them because we'd never seen it done. On the other hand, we didn't totally disbelieve them either, and that added an extra element of excitement.

On a recent trip to Felton Little Park, I found the slide and merry-go-round of my carefree youth were gone. Thank goodness the ancient clanking swings remained. Somehow you just can't improve on a swing. It's still the symbol of childhood when play is intense and wild and wonderful.

Lightning Bugs

Lightning bugs have returned with the hot weather, and on a dark moonless night they turn the back yard into a theater under the stars, like flickering rhinestones punched into a stark sheet of obsidian. In the summertime my clan-like family gets together at my mother's house. And for a while it's like it was when I was a little girl, except this go-'round I'm the older generation.

After supper I send my sister Jane out with the children figuring it takes less energy to wash a few dishes than to deal with five fidgety children between the ages of 3 and 8. Soon after they head outside, the little ones start running back into the kitchen one at a time, hands cupped together, frantically hollering, "Quick get me a jar, I've got a lightning bug!" All but 3-year-old Katherine. She's opts for a roly-poly instead of a firefly.

I resort to zip-lock baggies since all the Mason jars seem to have disappeared, and help each animated child transfer the insects into captivity. "You let it get away," D.J. moans. "Get it back." And I look helplessly at the light fixture way above my head and watch the bug flit around the artificial light.

"We'll get another one," I say and follow him outside into the scent of the pine-laden night air. A late afternoon toad strangler, a heavy rain that beat harshly on the window- panes, has cooled things off; and a soft breeze brushes against my face. I'm greeted by the happy shouts and shrieks of Seth and Ben and the rhythmic mime of Kristen gracefully chasing a bug. The sound of cricket legs rubbing together has a narcotic affect, and I start to almost believe I'm a kid again.

It's strange how much you can remember about past times once you let your mind wander on the trails that lead back. You remember one thing and that suddenly reminds you of something else.

I remember clearest of all those summer nights after supper playing in the humid Auburn air. After a hot day of serious fun—splashing in the murky water at Prather's Lake, day camp up on the mountain at Chewacla, or a pick-up game of softball at Felton Little Park—nighttime play was best of all.

While the grown-ups rocked on the porch cooling themselves with cardboard fans, Mama dished up home-churned ice cream or scooped store-bought lemon ice-milk from a carton. And just as children do these days, we laughed and ran and captured lightning bugs and stuffed them in jars.

Sambo, our black Cocker Spaniel, hopped around biting at bugs like a snapping turtle. His long ears flopping and stubby tail wagging, you'd swear he was grinning.

We hardly even noticed the steady swarm of dive-bombing mosquitoes until later when we were covered in whelps that itched us to death. And we sure weren't aware of the passing time. Not till Mama called us to come in. Then we'd beg, "Just five more minutes?"

Suddenly my musing is interrupted by those same pleas from today's younger generation as they're led away like prisoners on death row to waiting mini-vans. And as I stand wiggling my fingers "goodbye," the timelessness between us ends.

October Nights

It can't get much better than the soft, subtle breeze of a cool October twilight. Most evenings I walk with my two terriers at half past suppertime. Last night Chopper sporting his new harness stopped to water a weed, and a boy of about five called out, "Hey, that's my property!" I said, "Sorry." And he called back in his husky kid voice, "It's all right. A dog's gotta do his business." I laughed and moved on. Then I turned, watching him mount his small bicycle. As he pedaled in circles staying close to his house, I thought about all the Fall evenings I frittered away as a child.

Those early years in West Point, Georgia are about as clear as a windshield in a gully-washer. But I have a few sharp images of the crisp October nights. I recall riding my tricycle up and down the front walkway, pretending it was a Palomino stallion. And my sister Jane and I slipping under the "bob-wire" fence behind the house, chasing each other like mustangs in the pasture until we saw the bull. Then screaming and running for our lives, scooted back under the fence.

On Friday nights, Daddy took us to the high school football games. I wore my red West Point Red Devils sweat shirt and played under the bleachers with first grade friends, breathing in the musky smell of peanuts, almost oblivious to the background sounds of the snare drum, the referee's whistle, and high-pitched chanting of cheerleaders.

When we moved to Auburn, our nighttime shenanigans were much the same. Simple pleasures were all we had, and we dedicated ourselves avidly to self-imposed games. We caught lizards by the tail, or held roly-poly bugs in the palms of our hands watching them curl up into tight balls.

In October, the leaves were starting to turn from green to stunning colors—yellow, scarlet, and orange, beginning to break free from the dogwoods and oak trees. Soon there would be more than enough to stuff into a mesh potato sack to make a football. Until then, we'd play like we were in the World Series. I'd run inside, and on my knees, I burrowed through closets searching for a ball and bat. I'd finally pull out my wooden bat that was cracked at the neck. Then go on a quest for a bit of sticky electrical tape to wrap around the split, and I'd wind it up tight as I could with about half a roll of that black tape. After a rowdy game of pitch, catch, and hit— Jane and I made up the entire Brooklyn Dodger roster—we'd flop on our backs in the velvety carpet of zoysia grass under the street light. My dog Sambo rested his head on my stomach, and I scratched his ears while we gazed at the star-speckled sky and pretended we didn't hear Mama calling us to come in.

In hindsight, those long ago nights seem practically perfect.

Rites of Spring

Spring is a miracle whenever it happens to show up. Buds break, warbling wrens return, and green spreads softly over the land. It seems to hover in the air like wafting smoke with no particular destination in mind. Fresh fragrances cling to the air and children beg to go outside shoeless. You can't put a price tag on such things. They're available at no cost to CEO and bag lady alike.

When I was a little girl, winter always seemed eternal. "Won't spring ever come?" we'd whine. And finally it would happen. The smiling sun would start to beam and the air became soft and sweet. Walking home from school, we leaped over sidewalk puddles or splashed recklessly in them. We ran and shouted, suddenly gone crazy with spring. Sounds of children broke out everywhere: the slap of jump ropes, the flapping of home-made grocery-bag kites, and the chuckle of jacks on a smooth stone walk.

Then it was time to dig out my jingling bag of marbles. I'd root around listening to the metallic click, feeling the smooth, glass surface, and extract them one by one – Black beauties, Clearies, Aggies, Chalkies, and Glassies. We'd draw a circle in the dirt, deposit our marbles in the center, and knuckle down with the shooter. Sometimes we played "for keeps," carting off the booty like rare jewels. Other times we played "for fair," returning the captured marbles at the end of the game.

Spring meant plowing through clogged closets in search of roller skates. I'd check my old hand-me-downs by slapping the wheels and listening to the smooth, purring music of the spin. Then I'd find just the right piece of string to hang my skate key on. With skates clamped to hard-sole shoes and skate key dangling at my chest like an amulet, I glided up College Street to the railroad tracks. Then I'd step gingerly over metal cross-ties, squat and coast down the steep slope wind in my face, like a skier in the Alps. I intimately knew the neighborhood sidewalks. I learned to jump the cracks of old broken-down ones instead of clomping around them in the grass. I knew which ones were so bumpy they made my teeth rattle as I skimmed along. And I knew the stretches smooth as velvet where my wheels hummed as I gathered speed and the cross-cracks made a rhythmic clicking.

Sometimes I'd walk to the Dari-Delite on Gay Street and treat myself to a foot-long chilidog or a hot fudge sundae. One spring I got a catcher's mitt and mask to protect me from my sister Jane's killer fastballs. Nowadays there's nothing like the thud of a baseball slapping a leather mitt to take me back to those savory seasons of my youth.

Springtime Saturday afternoons at my Aunt Mary's house, the grown-ups loafed on the back porch while the children played with an old croquet set. The wooden balls having been chewed by dogs and eroded by rain were no rounder than dried up oranges. The paint was chipped and faded, and the wickets were bent out of any recognizable shape. We laid the course out on her tiny lawn happily and haphazardly, chose mallets, and played noisily with our cocker spaniel racing after the balls.

When I was a girl, I hung out in the trees every spring. These days I'm more prone to sitting on a park bench. Seems they don't make tree limbs as comfortable as they used to. But I can still sit back and sniff the scent of days gone by. Catch a whiff of honey suckle, take in a cantata of bird songs, and watch the children gone crazy with spring.

Spring Day

"The first day of spring is one thing, and the first spring day is another," Henry van Dyke said. "The difference between them is sometimes as great as a month."

He got that right. This year the first day of spring, the vernal equinox, came on March 20. But since then we've had delirious days of tornadoes, hail storms and ravaging rains. Not to mention it's been cold.

Real spring is that savory season that separates the cold, wet weather of winter from the hot weather of summer. When the green gets back in the trees, azaleas bloom and buttercups appear. Sturdy yellow daffodils are budding everywhere, roses scramble every which way over fences, red-clover shawls cover highway shoulders, and a tangle of wisteria and sweet-smelling honeysuckle paint everything in sight.

If you stay inside during the slow approach of warm weather, you're sure it will never come, because outside the window nothing seems to happen. But if you venture outside, you notice changes.

A slow walk on a spring day uncovers things you might have otherwise missed. Prowling through the green tangle in front of your nose, turning aside prickly branches. Freezing in your tracks as a snake slowly, methodically, zigzags from the roadside, down the slope and into the drainage ditch. Stooping to watch a snail sliding easily out of his shell-home. Glancing regretfully at your clean jeans, you plop to the ground, your knees sinking deep in pine straw so you can have a closer look.

In the springtime a walker has all kinds of wildlife for company, from an occasional turtle or lizard to squirrel and chipmunk patrols. Warm weather brings out various human specimens as well. Regular walkers recognize each other, sometimes nodding, exchanging a few pleasant words.

On the sidewalk there's an obstacle course of potholes and puddles. Walkers grin at each other as they dodge the splashes of joggers who run through the water. The green grass border is squishy underfoot, soggy in spots.

Walk in the late afternoon just before suppertime, pausing beneath tall trees, turning in slow circles, peering into the branches to discover a tiny titmouse amid the leaves. Spy on songbirds building nests in the bushes, pecking at grubs, or pulling worms from the dirt. Birds of every description. Cardinals, Carolina chickadees, bluebirds, and goldfinches.

In early spring there are times when I'm afraid to look the other way for fear I might miss some lovely and fleeting sight. Nearsighted, I squint and just barely focus on a flamboyant thicket of wildflowers.

As a girl, come spring I took to the trees. It was my private pleasure to scoot up a dogwood tree and settle comfortably among the branches in daily communion with its bark, leaves and buds. I was determined not to come down before I had to; if possible, never. Peering down through the young leaves, I could see buds closed as tightly as clinched fists. Another glance and they were beginning to unfurl. The next day they would be nearly open; the next, fully uncurled.

It's a little harder climbing trees these days. Middle-aged women aren't as agile as 10-year-old girls. And tree perching isn't socially acceptable for a grandmother. But don't be too surprised if you start up a dogwood tree and find a gray-haired woman yelling down at you, "Sorry, this tree is already taken!"

Winter Walk

Okay, so I might not make this statement if I lived in Minnesota. But the fact is, I like to walk in the wintertime. Depending on what day in January one reads this, he or she might write a letter of protest. "You like to walk when?"

Icy sleet may be falling, coating power lines, causing electrical outages. Once-a-year snow may be wilting the front-yard elephant's-ears or breaking stems of daffodils that had risked poking out into last week's sunshine.

Unseasonable warmth may have left everyone sweating and complaining, wondering about turning on the air-conditioning, while the azaleas open, droop, and die. The newspaper may have just heralded a new record: lows, highs, flooding or drought, late frost or early thaw.

Seems winter weather is unpredictable. Even in Alabama, unexpected things happen: blizzards, freezing rain, single digit temperatures that cause cars to cough and sputter.

Nonetheless, I took a walk this morning after breakfast. Not just an ordinary walk around my neighborhood on that infernal blacktop. This was a walk in the woods, exploring, watching, and listening.

The hardest part of a winter walk is getting out the front door. I pull on layers of clothes to fight off the frigid temperature. Long johns, T-shirt, sweats, down vest, jacket, double socks, duck boots, gloves and toboggan hat. I waddle out the door round as a penguin and drive to my favorite walking spot.

I park the car near my pony's pasture. I whistle and she meets me at the gate. I'm tempted to hop on Snicker's back but figure I need to use my own two feet. So I hook up her halter and lead rope and take her along.

We walk out along the fence row, past a fat-bellied mockingbird. We cross Serpentine Hill, skirting around prickly purple-and-green thistle and crusty ant hills. I stop and Snicker finds a clump of grass to munch on while I watch a family of field sparrows flit to the crotch of a wind-broken hardwood tree. The freezing air stings my face, and I hunker down deep into my clothing.

I turn onto a narrow woody trail and we tramp single file down a hill. Our six feet mash and crunch dead leaves and frozen moss. From the ice-covered brambles, come the high-pitched tweets of a lighthearted Wood Thrush. And in the other direction, the steady drone of a chainsaw. I hear busy rustlings in a briar patch and happily remember that it's wintertime— the season of reptile hibernation.

We step over fallen trees, dead and rotting, and slosh through a stream. The rippling water is as cold as a Root Beer float through my insulated boots, and sounds cheerful, almost musical, like crystal goblets clinking in a pan of sudsy dishwater. Then up a twisting trail, past a listless pond that looks like a perfect putting green with its thick coat of pea-green scum.

It's midmorning and the sun is gaining on me. A sheet of sweat forms, and I shed my coat. I want to follow one more path, but it's time to circle back.

Back at the barn I pour the little mare's daily ration of sweet feed into a black rubber bucket and throw two flakes of hay over the fence. She greedily gobbles up the grain but ignores the hay to stand at the gate watching me.

As I walk away, Snicker whinnies, calling me back. My old cynical self figures she's begging for more sweet feed. But the kid in me makes me turn and call out, "See ya, Snicker—see ya, little girl. I had fun too!" And I'm glad all over that I braved that winter walk.

The Light Side

"Laughter is an instant vacation."

Milton Berle

Flying

I was having a conversation with my son-in-law. He and I agree on most things. For instance, we both think his wife is gorgeous, brilliant and witty. And we're sure that his five children are the cutest and most clever tykes around.

We were discussing the one thing we disagree on—air travel. Problem is, he learned to fly one of those large metal tubes years ago, and he can quote all kinds of statistics about airplane safety. He says things like, "Did you know it's safer to fly than to walk to your mailbox?" Great! Now I'm scared to check the mail.

I don't have any statistics to back up my theories on flying. I rely strictly on gut feelings. If God had intended for man to fly, I say, He wouldn't have given us cars, buses, and road maps.

Let me make one thing perfectly clear. I am not afraid of flying. It's the crashing part that terrifies me. I'm not even afraid to die. It's just that I'd like to go peacefully in my sleep. Not careening out of control through the wild blue yonder. Not going faster than the speed of Superman toward an Idaho potato field.

I flew a while back for the first time in twenty years. It was the fault of sadistic friends and relatives who love to fly. They told me it would be all right. I was fine until I got to the Atlanta airport. The first thing I saw was a sign that said, "Terminal." And that started me wondering again.

As soon as we boarded the Boeing 747, the pilot's smooth voice came over the speaker. "Our flight will be delayed briefly while mechanics make a small repair," he told us. What kind of small repair, I wondered. And if you don't get a screw tight enough in a commercial jetliner, what happens? Anybody knows that if you break down in an automobile, you simply pull over, get out and call a wrecker.

"Is there an emergency lane for broken-down airplanes?" I asked my husband who was sitting next to me, calmly reading a newspaper.

"Relax. We'll be fine," he said.

I pretended to relax. For three hours I kept my eyes squeezed tight and my jaw clenched. My fingers gripped the armrests. Then the plane started to lose altitude. I opened one eye and peeped out the window. A piece of the wing flapped up.

In my calmest hysterical voice I told my husband, "This is it. The wing is falling off."

"Shhh. We're just landing," he said.

"But the wing…"

"That's supposed to go up. It helps slow the plane down. Look, there's Salt Lake City."

Then there was a bump. "What was that?" I moaned.

"We just landed," he said.

I peeped again. He was right. With my adrenaline back to normal, I walked to the exit. The smooth-voiced pilot was coming out of the cockpit. "Great flight!" I said confidently.

After my turbulent, bouncing and tossing trip back to Atlanta, I promised myself that I would never be cajoled, shamed or bullied into getting on another airplane. But I'm sure it's only a matter of time before the subject comes up.

"It's safer to fly than to eat at a salad bar," my son-in-law will say.

Too bad I'm not a Navajo Indian. A Navajo man isn't allowed to look at his mother-in-law much less try to talk some sense into her.

Household Hints

My daughter stopped letting me help with her homework when she discovered I thought a hypotenuse was a baby hippo. But she did allow me to make her school lunches on occasion.

I always packed lunches the night before, because early in the morning I had trouble remembering how many children I had left at home, and I was prone to make the wrong number of sandwiches. But at eleven o'clock at night, I'm in full possession of my faculties.

What I don't possess late at night is something to make a sandwich with, unless you count a jar of what I think is grape jam. Then again, it could be the salve I bought to rub on the dog's dry skin.

I stare into the refrigerator as if I were watching a rerun of my favorite "Masterpiece Theater." They say that before you die, events from your life flash before your eyes. I don't know if this is true, never having died, but I've found that when I root around in the refrigerator, memories of past months whiz by.

I remember a friend who, in a pinch, made a tasty sandwich spread by mixing cream cheese and yogurt with chili powder. I lack the creativity to invent that kind of concoction. For that matter, I lack the sour cream and chili powder.

I know this is an admission of failure. I've tried reading books of household hints, but they never seem to work for me. Over the years, thousands of hints have sifted like uncooked grits through my fingers. So I speak with a certain amount of authority when I say that most household hints are pretty lame. They suggest:

*When you burn yourself in the kitchen, vanilla will help ease the pain. They don't mention whether you should apply it or drink it.

*It's handy to keep a soft powder puff in the flour bin for dusting cake pans. I gave this up when my cakes tasted like Jean Nate and my body was covered with All-Purpose Pillsbury.

*Your sewing needles slide easily and never rust if you keep them stuck in a bar of soap in your sewing box. Since I can barely fit a needle in my stamp-sized sewing kit, I can't for the life of me figure out how I'm supposed to get a bar of soap in there too.

Maybe I should write my own book of household hints. My advice would be much more practical. Things like:

*If you own a shaggy dog and are tired of vacuuming the floors and furniture, just vacuum the dog.

*When you're heading out the door and notice your hem has come out, stapling is a quick fix. It lasts longer than Scotch tape, and people probably won't even notice all the tiny holes that are left.

*If you're overwhelmed with stress, some say grab a Hershey Bar. Seems chocolate has the same effect as Prozac. Truth is, I've found a better stress reliever—the primal scream.

How to Buy a Bathing Suit

I'm tired of all this nonsense about character being more important than beauty. If that were the case there wouldn't be all those magazine articles insisting that I can be a younger, lovelier me this summer.

Actually I've been intending to be a younger, lovelier me for years, but with one thing and another—we had to have the house re-roofed, and the dog developed recurring bladder stones—I never got around to it. Now here it is spring again, time to think about a new bathing suit for the beach.

I want to make it perfectly clear that I'm not all that concerned with my appearance. But when I make a trip to the ocean, I want something to wear out on the beach that's a little more fashionable than my old beige raincoat.

Last time I shopped for beach attire I marched bravely into Dillard's and stood for a while in a corner studying the salesladies. What I didn't want was an attractive, aggressive saleslady. I finally selected a mousy matron who seemed a little shy. I went boldly over to her, pulled out a picture of a young Esther Williams in a sensible, one-piece suit and blurted out, "I want to look like this." Of course, I was referring to the swimsuit, but she eyed the glimmering body of the athletic super-star, the long, lean limbs, and smiled smugly. "Hon, we all do. But a mountain climber doesn't start with Mt. Everest."

This year I was determined to take the offensive. I headed for the mall to rummage through the early glut of swimming attire. Some weren't too bad, but others seemed smaller than the price tags dangling from them.

I scanned the one-piece section, skillfully dodging helpful salespeople before they could discretely size up my backside. After all, I know a thing or two about fashion.

I found just the right thing, a black suit with white vertical stripes. Just to make sure, I grabbed a couple more suits. A royal blue number, because that's a good color on me, and a brown one with polka dots.

In the dressing room, I pulled and twisted the elastic material over my hips then vetoed each snug suit when I looked in the wall-to-wall mirrors. In the black and white I resembled a young zebra. The blue reminded me of the blueberry girl in "Willie Wonka," and in the brown polka-dotted one, I was a dead ringer for a raisin-bran muffin.

I kept up my search until I started thinking in a Dr. Seuss-like gibberish, "Too glitzy, too frilly, too skimpy, too silly. Too matronly, too lumpy, too plain, too frumpy." And in the end I came away with yet another ill-purchased swimsuit that I'll never actually wear.

Problem is, what do you do with a drawer full of unused bathing suits? They can't be sent to flood victims in Honduras or to the deserving poor. They don't even make good dust rags.

From now on, I'm going to stop struggling with this whole younger, lovelier me business and work on developing my character. I'm going to march straight back into that store and buy something different to wear on the beach, something decent and comfortable—a new beige raincoat.

Learning to Spell

I may be the fourth grade teacher's worst nightmare. This came to mind the other day when someone asked me, "What's your favorite weird word?" Of course, I was ready with a roster of favorite weird words.

This lineup of unusual words in my memory was due to my youngest daughter's education. Mary Beth was part of the time in which the child was supposed to discover her own path to enlightenment. In kindergarten, her school used the "whole language" approach. A big part of a student's learning to read required listening to stories, drawing pictures and writing as many sounds as she could in her journal. Each morning one child would share an experience for the rest of the children to record. At the beginning of the year, the entries were heavy on pictures with a random letter or two. But as time went on, there were less drawings and more letters and eventually lots of words with an occasional bit of artwork. And, yes, Mary Beth became a good reader by the end of the year.

The whole language approach was still popular when she got to the fourth grade. The way to teach spelling that year was the "have-a-go" method. The teacher read out a word, and the child would have a go at spelling it. Then the teacher checked the spelling and if it wasn't correct, which was most of the time, she'd send the child to a dictionary to have another go at it. This continued until the proper spelling was determined.

One day Mary Beth came home with a combined spelling/vocabulary assignment. Each child was to choose her own spelling words, look up the definition, and write a sentence with each one.

This is where I entered the picture with my favorite weird words. I figured most of the kids would pick drab, monosyllable words. It would just be time wasted on a dreary piece of busy work. I had a better plan. I insisted on picking the words myself, and to really cheat the system, I'd find words that were not only amusing and interesting, but easy to spell. No tricky combinations of letters or confusing "i-before-e" words. I carefully selected boisterous, ambiguous, enigma, whippersnapper, insidious, verbose, intrinsic, ominous, and, my favorites humdrum, flabbergasted, disgruntled, and discombobulated. She had fun with the assignment, making up unusual sentences. The teacher was puzzled by Mary Beth's glossary of words and impressed that she could spell them.

That all happened several years ago. I'm proud to say that my daughter graduated Magna Cum Laude from Auburn University, and she maintained a 4.0 GPA while earning her master's degree from the University of South Carolina. She's also a much better speller than I am, although my education was the traditional kind. And, I'm glad to report that she's never humdrum, rarely flabbergasted and is downright "gruntled" and "combobulated" most of the time.

Never-Fail Diets

If beauty is as beauty does, why are the bookstores bulging with best-selling diet books? And speaking of bulging, that term could apply to most American's too. Diets and diet books are a three billion dollar market in the U.S.

It's a funny thing that all of us want to be thin, but at the same time we can't stop stuffing our faces with chocolate-filled doughnuts.

A recent news story told about a man who weighed 1,000 pounds. When he got sick, he had to be airlifted to the hospital in a sling used for baby whales. Reporters believed the man weighed more than any other living human. I can only say, I hope so.

Another weight-related story told about a man who claimed to have lost 1,000 pounds in his lifetime. Problem was, every time he lost weight he gained it back. So, naturally, he's suing the companies that promoted the weight loss programs.

You can't blame the man. It certainly isn't his fault that he has no will power. If these weight loss programs are going to help us lose weight, the least they can do is force us to keep it off.

I've lost at least 1,000 pounds in my time, and as an overweight American I'd like to say something about diets. I'm sick of them. I've tried them all:

"The All-Prune Diet."

"How Talk Show Hosts Lost Weight Eating Pure Lard."

" Take Off pounds with the Amazing Blackberry Seed Diet."

"The Juicy Fruit Chewing Gum Diet That Can't Fail."

"Why Having Your Lips Stitched is a Sure Way to Shed Pounds."

A sample daily diet reads like this:

BREAKFAST:
One white grape
½ slice zwieback
5 oz. decaffeinated, unsweetened tea (room temperature)

LUNCH:
Two white grapes
Six bites of tuna (in spring water)
Four grams of fat-free pretzels
Two sniffs of a Snickers candy bar

DINNER:
¾ cup plain tofu
Two oz. boiled, chopped chicken liver
32 grains of brown rice
3-tsp. banana pudding—custard, meringue and wafers removed.

Thumb through any magazine or newspaper and you're sure to find a new, fool-proof, delicious way to lose weight without giving up any of your favorite foods. Of course, this only works if your favorite foods happen to be raw asparagus, fat-free curds, sugar-free Jell-O, and shaved ice with two squirts of artificial lemon juice.

Unlike some of my friends who think Angelina Jolie is fat, I prefer the full-figured look. I remember the fat-friendly '50s when everyone admired the pleasantly padded profiles of Debbie Reynolds and Doris Day. Back then miniskirts were worn only by little girls under the age of four or Scottish soldiers.

I wish people would quit saying that beauty is only skin deep. I feel we should go deeper. I'm quite sure I have a perfectly adorable pancreas.

Speech

Sometimes I read British mysteries. And when I do, I'm amazed at how much we've altered the English language. Seems we don't speak English at all.

We wait in lines. The British stand in queues. We call or phone. They ring up. Our cars have tires, mufflers, windshields, trunks and hoods. Their motor vehicles have tyres, silencers, windscreens, boots and bonnets. We use gas. They use petrol. We have flashlights. They have torches. Americans mail packages. The British post parcels.

But there's an even greater discrepancy between American dialect and Southern jargon. Southern speech is much more colorful and descriptive. We try never to say with one word what we can say with two.

We use a dish rag in the kitchen and a wash rag in the bath tub. For grooming we have hair brushes, and instead of moisturizers there's cold cream. To cover up a shiny nose we use face powder.

We zip up pants, fill up water glasses, fix up the spare room, wash up the dishes, eat up the leftovers, climb up the stairs and tear up paper. And we never reverse. We back up. We don't do research. We read up on a subject. A house either burns up or burns down. And we sit down, turn around, and jump off of, out of, on, over, up or down. Sweaters don't shrink in the dryer. They draw up.

Our cars don't come with accelerators. They have gas pedals. For outside watering we use hose pipes. And red bugs, not chiggers, make us itch to death.

If Southerners lose something, we wouldn't be caught dead searching. We'd hunt for it or look all over the place for it. If we're tired we say we're tuckered out, or give out. And we're never annoyed. We have pet peeves.

Our expressions of surprise go way beyond golly or gee. We prefer: my word, well I'll say, have mercy, I'll swanee, or great gobs of goose grease.

Instead of saying, "He almost died," we say, "He liked to have died." And we much prefer greeting a friend with, "Hey there," rather than "Hi" or "Hello." If a neighbor comes calling, we don't ask them to come in, we tell them to come in the house.

Our foods are descriptive too. We eat light bread, table salt, black pepper, sliced tomatoes, layer cake, table syrup, sweet tea, and sweet milk.

Even weather conditions are described with colorful phrases. If it rains, it's a gully washer or toad strangler. In the summertime, it's not just hot, it's hot enough to fry an egg on the sidewalk.

Northerners go to the market and push a buggy while selecting vegetables.

Southerners go over to the grocery store and push a grocery cart while they pick out a mess of collard greens.

Wish I could chew the fat a while longer, but I'm fixin' to have to go.

Critters

"Animals are such agreeable friends—
they ask no questions;
they pass no criticisms."

George Eliot

Back in the Saddle

"Not bad for a grandmother," my friend yelled as I trotted around the make-shift riding ring on her chubby Palomino Haflinger. I appreciated the vote of confidence, but I'll have to admit it blurred my image of me as Roy Rogers cantering across the prairie on Trigger.

My earliest memories include dreams of horseback riding. But my only experience with a live horse came the summer I was five. Daddy rented a horse for a month for my sister Jane and me while we were spending the summer at our cabin on the river. I usually rode double with Jane, but one day as I perched on his bare back, he took off up the hill. I thought he was at a dead run. In truth, he was probably walking fast. I bounced up and down like the lid of a teakettle holding on for all I was worth while my whole family chased us into the bushes.

Twenty years later when I moved to Virginia and started taking riding lessons, a friend encouraged me to ride her big chestnut Thoroughbred, Rosie. I was less than confident about riding the high-strung mare, but she insisted Rosie was gentle. So, one morning I threw on a saddle, tightened her girth and mounted. We walked up the dirt road and crossed a lush green lawn, and I remembered to sit back a notch going down the steep slope. As soon we reached the bottom of the hill, we were on the road to the nearby waterfront. I was feeling more confident now, but still alert. When we made it to the sandy strip of beach on the Rappahannock River, my relief turned to a cocky feeling of assurance. I dropped my feet from the stirrups and loosened the reins, holding onto the buckle with two fingertips. I nudged Rosie, heading her into the brackish river.

My plan was to stand in the shallow water for a few minutes. Rosie had other ideas. She whipped around and headed up the road at a gallop. And this time it really was a dead run. I managed to get my feet back in the stirrups and shortened my reins. But the Thoroughbred had her head. There was no way I'd get control of her. My goal was to stay on, but I knew I had to do something fast. Heavy trucks barreled along the blacktop up ahead. A thick forest of loblolly pines loomed on my right. The only option was to get to the steep slope on my left by making a sharp turn at a gallop and immediately jumping a three-foot ditch. So, with my eyes closed, that's what I did. We made it across, and Rosie slowed to a trot. She stopped at the top of the hill, and I got off and led her home.

You'd think that I would have given up riding. Instead, I bought a horse, became a decent rider, and even taught lessons before I quit. And now, all these years later, I'm happily back in the saddle again.

Barn Cats

Thirty years of horse owning has thrown me unwittingly in contact with creatures totally unlike equines. I'm referring, of course, to a breed of felines commonly called barn cats.

Barn cats aren't like ordinary cats. They are Bengal tigers in a smaller form. Their ancestors were saber-toothed. They are sly and quick; prowlers in the night, tracking puffs of mouse-breath.

Barn cats are the product of two mutually exclusive impulses. First, an unequaled instinct for survival, and second, a compulsion toward personal injury.

These two opposing forces come together in barn cats. That's because the cat, more than any other living creature, takes absolute pleasure in lethargy. While other animals live to eat, like cows; to fly, like pigeons; or to multiply, like rabbits; the cat finds no greater meaning in life than to wallow in ceaseless, uninterrupted sleep.

No other animal has a body so conducive to sleep. Happening upon a log, rock, cast-off tire or bramble bush, a cat will make it a bed.

Since slothfulness is the Achilles Heal of barn cats, these students of the horizontal can usually be found in a warm space slumbering. Unfortunately, the warmest site isn't always the safest. For instance, one of the warmest spots on a farm is on top of an electric motor. A soft, massaging heat emanates from tractor motors providing luxury beyond the finest Jacuzzi. The problem is that the cat has a tail, and electric motors connected to belts and fans love anything that protrudes. The result is a tail-stub, similar in appearance to a sawed-off shotgun.

Another dangerous warm spot is a bed of sun-baked hay. Once the critter has staked out his claim on a pile of heated hay, it's next to impossible to make him move over for a hungry horse. Any idiot knows that a mound of horse-hay doesn't make a good sleeping spot. Connected to the pony are hooves and teeth. But cats think they can recline in the comfort of a perilous place until the last possible moment. They count on having time to skedaddle before an ear is mistaken for fodder or a restless foot smashes a skull.

I owned a pregnant cat that made a nest for her babies under a heap of hay in a horse trailer. Refusing to budge when time came to haul a gelding to a two-day show in Florida, she hid so nobody knew she was there until the trailer crossed the state line. She survived the trip and had the kittens as soon as she got back to Auburn.

For the most part, the farm cat can't get entirely killed by accidents alone. But by definition a true barn cat has carved away unnecessary appendages and organs. In the fall a foot is lost to the hay mower. During the spring an eye is surrendered to a blue jay in a territorial standoff. In winter, half the hide is sacrificed.

The genuine barn cat has three legs, one eye, and so much fur missing from its backside, it resembles a hairless Chihuahua. But with the loss of each body part, the kitty's wit rises. The wise barn cat eventually learns that the warmest spot isn't always the best choice. And in the end he's as good as immortal.

Cool Air Birds

I'm sitting at my computer in the study, and I get a text from my daughter Emily who's in the kitchen. "You have some traveling birds," she says, and I text her back. "How do you know?" I wait a minute, and get the reply. "I rarely see 5 different kinds of birds visiting." "I'm jealous!" I text her, getting up and heading for the kitchen window.

But of course, by the time I get there they're gone. I stand there, disappointed, squinting at the bushes. And I remember reading that as fall migration approaches, the birds that migrate even short distances have to bulk up to sustain themselves on their journey. So I wait, knowing that visits to feeders will pick up.

As I lean against the sink, peering through the screen, I recall a morning last December. It was a glorious day for watching birds. My birds had been scarce since I'd gotten back from my Thanksgiving vacation—ten days of bird-drought. During those sparse mornings, I'd seen a Blue Jay or two and an occasional red-robed Cardinal.

That morning had been frigid, in the low 20s—the coldest we'd had so far. The water in my faux birdbath was solid. My usual trick of bashing the ice with a big rock didn't make a dent. I picked up the green flowerpot-base that held the frozen water and smacked it on the ground. No dice. So I went inside and filled a large plastic Subway cup with hot tap water and took it outside, pouring it over the ice. Steam rose up like fog on a Smoky Mountain morning.

A dozen sassy Blue Jays—a whole extended family—swooped and dived from one feeding station to the next, banging into each other like little boys in bumper cars, then moving on. They pushed and shoved at the birdbath like a hot day at the water cooler.

One lone brilliantly red Cardinal hunkered under the wicker feeder picking up Blue Jay crumbs. A gutsy Tufted Titmouse darted onto the window ledge where I'd scattered two fists-full of wild bird seed, quickly poking it's beak into the mix. And somewhere in the tree branches a tiny Carolina Chickadee waited for her chance. Then out of the literal blue, there was a red-bellied Woodpecker. He challenged the Jays unafraid, flitting from feeder to feeder and helped himself to water. And as all the local woodpeckers seem to do, he staked out the basketball goal's wooden backboard, stuffing past-hammered holes with seed for a mid-morning snack.

My reminiscing stops at the sound of an ill wind blowing from the east rattling limbs. It's growing dark fast. Against the windows, windblown rain pelts like buckshot. I reluctantly head back to my study to write. There'll be no more visiting birds this morning.

Dogs I've Loved

"Animals are such agreeable friends," the writer George Eliot said. I think dogs may be the most agreeable of all.

In my lifetime, I've had all different sizes, shapes, colors and breeds of dogs. And like George Bernard Shaw, "I like a bit of a mongrel." But what matters most is that the pup is a good companion.

When I watched the Westminster Dog Show on television not long ago I was interested to learn that Best in Show goes to the dog with the most poise and personality. My dogs have never lacked personality, but none has been blessed with a lot of poise. Along with their endearing traits, usually came an Achilles paw.

There was Lady, a Chow, who let my sister Jane and me dress her in my outgrown clothes and push her around in a baby carriage. And Whitey, a white German Shepherd who appeared in our yard one morning while I was riding my tricycle and refused to leave. Rufus M., a small white African Bush mix, had the wrinkled brow and tight-curled tail of a Basenji. This bark-less pooch had a constant smile, and he never got tired of jumping up and down.

Sambo, our flop-eared Cocker Spaniel, saw as a puppy that he was going to lead a dog's life—unless he stopped being a dog. So he decided to act like a human being. When we left him overnight at the Auburn University Small Animal Clinic, the doctor called saying, "Sambo escaped and is on his way home."

Riding in the car did strange things to Frodo, my Beagle/Australian Terrier. He perched wild-eyed and trembling on the back of the front seat, drooling down my neck. But he insisted on going to ride.

And while some dogs scratch at the door to be let in, Patches, a tri-colored Cocker Spaniel, raised his head and howled the shrill, doleful cry of an Alaskan timber wolf when he wanted in.

Little Miss Muffet, my first Miniature Schnauzer, like Sambo concluded that there was no future in being a dog, and she took on many human characteristics. She snored when she slept and burped after she ate. When Muffet was in the throes of a false-pregnancy, she produced milk and nursed a nearly newborn stray kitten I'd brought home from the barn.

George H. W. Bush's dog Millie apparently had more personality than poise too. In 1989 when she gave birth to four puppies, Bush was banished to Lincoln's bedroom because, "the dog refuses to go to the dog house."

The thing about dogs is, unlike children, they never resist naptime. They aren't embarrassed if you sing in public, and they don't care if the peas have touched the mashed potatoes. Best of all, as Aldous Huxley said, "To his dog, every man is Napoleon." I'd love to be the person my dogs think I am.

Marmalade

What's orange and white and weighs three-and-a-half pounds? It can leap over tall tables in a single bound, race through the house faster than the Road Runner, spin more swiftly than a ballerina on steroids, and out-nap Dagwood Bumstead. Give up? It's my daughter Emily's kitten, Marmalade.

Cats have always intrigued me—from the toughest tiger in Bangladesh to the tiniest house kitten. Cleaning their fur with pink emery board tongues. Purring, pouncing, clawing and climbing. Finally, they curl up in a fuzzy ball and doze.

Archaeologists have found evidence that I'm not the only one fascinated by cats. Seems they've been kept by humans for quite a while. An 8,700-year-old cat tooth was found at Jericho.

There's overwhelming evidence that points to Egypt as the place where cats were first domesticated. They probably entered early farming villages along the Nile to hunt river rats infesting granaries. More than 300,000 embalmed cats were found buried in an underground sanctuary built about 1400 BC. The temple, dedicated to the cat goddess Bastet, contained mummified mice beside the cases of cat mummies—food for the cat's journey to the afterworld.

During the 6th century BC, the Greek writer, Aesop, used cats in his fables. Cats have appeared in literature ever since, from the French fairy tale *Puss in Boots* to the recent *The Cat Who…* mysteries featuring Koko and Yum Yum, two sleuthing Siamese cats.

We've seen funny felines in "Arlo and Janis," "Sylvester," "Tom and Jerry" and "Garfield." Film cats were in "That Darn Cat," "Rhubarb," and "Thomasina." And Broadway honored felines in the play "Cats." Egyptian wall paintings from 1500 BC pictured cats. Painters Leonardo da Vinci, Chardin, Manet and Renoir included cats in their artwork. And local artist Barbara Keel specializes in cat pastels.

It's fun to watch Marmalade do the things that are common to cats. He perches on the back of a stuffed chair and turns the wheel of the 100-year-old spinning wheel my grandmother used to spin cotton thread. And he loops his tail around a bedpost batting at it as if it weren't attached to his body.

Sometimes I feel guilty when he sits in the windowsill and looks longingly at the outside world. But he's an indoor cat. There are too many dangers outside. Plus, there have been disputes about cats roaming around unrestrained.

In 1949, Illinois Gov. Adlai Stevenson vetoed a bill that would confine cats to the owner's property. "To escort a cat on a leash is against the nature of the cat," Stevenson said. "Moreover, cats perform useful services in combating rodents. We are interested in protecting birds, but the problem of cat versus bird is as old as time. If we attempt to resolve it by legislation, we may be called on to take sides as well in the age-old problem of dog versus cat or even bird versus worm."

For the time being, Marmalade will have to be content staying inside stalking the wild dust bunnies.

Sambo

I stumbled on a snapshot of him not long ago, his funny black face, his gentle eyes, his matted ears hanging low. As I studied the faded photo taken with a Brownie box camera 50-something years ago, I pondered the volumes that have been written about boys and their dogs as if the two went together like pancakes and cane patch syrup. And it crossed my mind that no boy ever loved a dog more than I loved Sambo.

I've had a slew of dogs in my life, but Sambo was my first, and none of those others ever quite measured up to him. I was four years old when he was born on the big front porch of our house in West Point, Georgia.

I remember the sweet smell of his puppy breath as his moist pink tongue licked all over my face. Then he'd wriggle, nuzzle my hand with his damp nose and fall asleep in the crook of my knee. My sister Beth owned the mama dog, a Cocker Spaniel, and she promised my sister Jane and me that we could have the pick of the litter.

To us, the pick of the litter was also the runt of the litter, a tiny bundle of soft, tar-black fuzz. We chose him at once and named him Little Black Sambo, a name that today would be politically incorrect, but we didn't know any better in those days.

We grew up alongside each other in that unhurried, out-of-the-way town. He bonded so completely with Jane and me that I'm sure he never knew he was a dog at all. Wherever we went, Sambo followed. We were a threesome, pretty much inseparable.

Sambo was still a young dog when we moved to Auburn. Back then Auburn was a quiet, lazy college town. That was before progress came calling, cutting down trees, raising up mega-stores and affluent subdivisions. On Saturday mornings Jane, Sambo and I scampered up North College Street to the Tiger Theater. Sambo waited patiently outside while we watched Roy Rogers or the Lone Ranger tame the West.

In the afternoon we'd walk to Felton Little Park. We splashed in the stream that trickled sluggishly under the bridge, and we followed each other down the big slide sitting on waxed paper so we'd go faster. Sambo climbed the tall ladder right behind us and zipped down the slide on his bottom with his ears sticking straight out.

I've never known a dog with such a downright dislike for dog food. Scoop a can of Friskies into his bowl and he'd turn up his nose and sulk back to his private spot on the family-room sofa. Otherwise he had a long list of favorite foods that included mashed potatoes and gravy, Parker House rolls, watermelon, butter-and-sugar sandwiches that we shared on the back stoop after school, meat loaf, green beans, fried corn bread, corned beef hash and Tootsie Rolls.

Sambo enjoyed traveling by car. In the fall and winter when the windows were rolled up, he sprawled out on the back ledge of the car, the shelf we called the doggie seat. But when warm weather hit and the windows were down, he stood on his back paws and leaned out the window. Sometimes he would hang so far out that nothing was left of him in the car except his hind feet and tail. And he would balance precariously, his nose thrust out and his long ears flapping in the breeze.

As I got older the years went by fast. Before I knew it Sambo had become quite old, close to 100 in dog years. When he died we buried him in our back yard.

E.B. White said, "A really companionable and indispensable dog is an accident of nature. You can't get it by breeding for it, and you can't buy it with money. It just happens along."

Of all the various dogs I've had, the best by far was the first, the one that happened along when I was a very little girl.

Saying Goodbye

In the middle of an August heat wave I went outside to feed the birds and was hit with an October-like breeze, cool and soft and invigorating. It was so out of season I wondered if I could be imagining it, conjuring up a pleasant feeling so I could face the day.

Sometimes days that start out full of hope turn sad. Less than 24 hours earlier, Muffin, my daughter Emily's tabby-co cat showed symptoms of critical sickness. I found a veterinary practice that was open on Sunday and drove her there. Hours of tests, and tubes, and antibiotics followed. She didn't respond to treatment and during the night had a full-blown seizure. So we were faced with the decision of whether or not to euthanize her.

Muffin came to us eleven years ago when I wasn't looking for a kitten. We already had a calico cat and a Schnauzer. But my niece called, pleading. She couldn't find a home for the runt of her mama cat's litter. It was a hopeless situation, she assured me. Then came the clincher. "Emily would love her."

I'd forgotten how tiny a 6-week-old kitten was until she came to us a miniscule handful of striped, swirled and dotted fuzz. Muffin stayed petite as she grew, but she became the alpha-pet, ruling both animals and humans. Like most cats there was a certain haughtiness to her graceful, aristocratic demeanor. But she had endearing traits that were strictly her own. Over the years Emily bought her all sorts of toys that rang, buzzed and hummed. The one she was devoted to was a three-inch crab made of orange cloth. She carried it from room to room where I invariably stepped on it.

When Emily practices her Special Olympics gymnastics, she plays songs that go with each routine. Not long ago I noticed those tunes playing at odd and random times. "Why are you playing your rhythmic music now?" I asked Emily.

"I'm looking for Muffin," she told me. "She comes when the music starts. She likes to exercise with me." I watched one day. As soon as the CD started, Muffin appeared from behind the couch, stretching and rolling while Emily went through her reps.

The day that had started with such promise ended on a horribly sad note. We stood by Muffin as she lay on a cushion, too weak and limp to lift her head. We petted and talked to her, and finally Emily said it was time. We waited while the pink sleeping-potion ended the life of the huntress who'd never ventured out of doors. After the tenderhearted doctor passed her stethoscope over Muffin's ribs and said, "She's gone," we stayed and stroked some more.

Years ago, I read a verse by Irving Townsend, "We who choose to surround ourselves with lives even more temporary than our own live within a fragile circle."

I should never have waited this long to discover how much I cared about that waif of a cat.

Worldly Goods

"There's never enough of the stuff you
can't get enough of."

Patrick Doyle

Attic to Attic

I'm growing more nostalgic with each passing day. I didn't mean for that to happen. I figured by middle age I'd be thick-skinned as a cobra, dulled, standing on the curb yawning as the band passed by. Played out, uninterested. That's what I thought.

Instead, I've taken to tugging on the dangling cord of the pull-down ladder that leads to the attic. I clamber up the steps like a noisy 10-year-old on a rainy day and rummage through great boxes bulging with a lifetime of souvenirs. Thick, plush photograph albums, fastened with decaying strands of leather infested with dry-rot. Bundles of string-tied letters. Saran-wrapped locks of hair. Maps marked with remembered routes of camping trips out West. Yellowed newspaper clippings falling apart from folding and refolding. Theater programs and match covers older than Leonardo DiCaprio.

I listen to the secret attic sounds. A squirrel skittering along the eaves. A pine branch tickling the shingles. The wind wheezing by. And on rainy days the staccato rhythm of droplets on the roof, steady as artillery fire.

Used to be, I'd rush to the attic to find some specific book like *Hop on Pop*. Then I'd hurdle back down, jumping past the last few rungs. Now I sit and pore over postcards trying to decide if I should frame this one or that one.

It occurred to me not long ago that maybe I should buy a filing cabinet for mementos I'll never use but can't stand to toss out. Under "A" would be artwork—those stacks of little drawings by my children. Sketches done in colored pencils, watercolors, and finger paints.

The "B" section would hold heaps of baby pictures too abundant to paste in albums.

And under "C" would be college memorabilia. Rooting through reminders of my college days opens a floodgate of memories. They come hurling at me like Tom Glavin fastballs. A time capsule discovered.

That first summer quarter. Band practice was at one o'clock in the afternoon in a steamy cracker-box room on the second floor of the old Music Building. We were smushed together like a tin of Toll House cookies that were stacked before they cooled.

Most of the other classrooms were just as hot. Math upstairs in Broun Hall and English in the L Building. Nothing was air-conditioned, and we couldn't wear shorts to class in those days.

Between classes, we drove past Chewacla to the rock quarry where we floated in the forbidden icy water. We cruised Opelika Road, scarfing fast food from Bonanza Burger, Hungry Boy and Dairy Delite. And late at night we'd meet at the Kopper Kettle for a cup of over-cooked coffee and a slab of coconut cream pie.

Four years of bull session, football games, classes, plays, band trips, fraternity parties, labs, road trips, coffeehouse readings, lectures, exams, movies and concerts.

Greedy as a chipmunk with a jaw full of nuts, I pulled the pieces of my past from cardboard boxes I've toted from attic to attic for safekeeping. If I move, I'll take the boxes along, make room for them in the new house's attic, because their contents matter, because they make me smile.

I'll take them because I can't leave them behind. I know it to be true, for dead certain.

Beetle

Man, how I loved that car. It was light mint green. And it had the lines of a fat lady in the circus. It had running boards and four-on-the-floor, and the lawnmower-sized engine was in the rear.

I was eighteen when my daddy bought me my first car. He said I could choose whatever I wanted, within reason. I was used to driving his big Ford Galaxy, but of course, I wanted a Volkswagen Beetle, a Bug.

When I drove it out of the VW dealer's parking lot, I immediately sat straighter and taller, and I felt like Sandra Dee or maybe Annette Funicello.

Back then Auburn University freshmen couldn't drive on campus, but somehow Daddy got my Bug registered. When I scooted from class to class, I had the feeling that every eye was on me and that I was God's gift to mankind, if only for the moment.

I took road trips to Panama City and New Orleans. Then one summer, I went on a cross-country camping trip to San Francisco with some friends. There was just enough room inside the car for the four of us, so our tents, cooking gear, and clothes were tied to the top and front of the tiny Beetle. We called it our covered wagon—Volkswagen, that is.

We headed down Route 66 in the summer heat with the windows wide open because VWs weren't air-conditioned in those days. That led to some unfortunate happenings beyond mere sweating—like the time a bird hit the windshield and landed in my lap dead.

I'm sure we must have gotten on each other's nerves cooped up in that hot box. But I mainly remember cooking barbecued chicken at the Grand Canyon, talking to Native Americans in Taos, New Mexico, and the brakes starting to go out as we descended a mountain into Death Valley.

I think of all this now because of the current crisis in the automobile industry. I'm no expert in marketing, but I've owned more than my share of cars. And I'm a firm believer in driving a car with character. I like having a vehicle that makes me smile when I look out the window and see it parked in my driveway.

These days I drive a car that looks good, is comfortable, and gets great gas mileage. But it doesn't give me a thrill.

Unfortunately, all cars look alike these days. In the past year, I've tried to get into a variety of small silver sedans—a Volvo, Mercedes, Honda, and Toyota. Each time I was surprised to discover that it wasn't my Hyundai Elantra. I long for a car I can glimpse at a distance and know that it's mine.

If I can scrape up the purchase price of a refurbished VW Bug, you might just spot me scooting around town, sitting straight and tall, thinking every eye is on me and that I'm God's gift to mankind, if only for a moment.

Brownie Box Camera

Back in the days when black-and-white snapshots ruled the world of photography, my daddy bought me a Brownie box camera. Man how I loved that camera. I carried the black box everywhere, clinging to the handle, taking candids of family, friends and dogs.

I'd stand a squinting sister in front of a dogwood tree or try to catch my mother unaware as she kneaded a mound of dough and pinched off Parker House Rolls. I'd pose Sambo the cocker spaniel or Rufus the smiling Basenji-mix on a step and click a few frames until I got just the right shot. Fact is, I tried to photograph anything that wasn't moving. There was no automatic advance. It was all click, twist, twist, click, turn, turn.

I took that square box of a camera to school and captured candids at recess. Not long ago I discovered a shoebox crammed with black-and-white, 2 x 3-inch prints. Sifting through the photos I dredged up some of those school days shots. On the playground, giggling grammar school girls posed in full felt Poodle skirts. Fifth grade tough guys flexed their muscles for the camera.

Later photos were indoor snaps of spend the night parties. It had taken practice to pop out the hot crinkled flashbulb and insert a fresh one in time to catch laughing, dancing, singing, eating, teenaged girls in baby doll pajamas. Girlish heads poking out from chin-high blankets, hair wrapped around plastic rollers the size of toilet paper spools.

Having my film developed was an adventure. One-hour processing was unheard of and film couldn't be mailed off. So I headed downtown to Manning Studio in a sprawling loft next to the Pitts Hotel on East Magnolia Avenue. The narrow stairway that led to the shop was long and dark and creaked under my shoes. It took some courage to climb those stairs alone, film clutched in my sweaty fist.

Mr. Manning did all the work right there. On the worktable were big, shallow, enamel pans for his negatives and prints, acetic acid, alum, and all the paraphernalia of his trade. 8 x 10 glossy photos spotted the walls showing lines of little girls with bobby pin curls wearing white or light-colored organdy and dotted swiss; or a gap-toothed boy, hair wetted down and parted, frozen in the photo like a butterfly pinned to cardboard.

I never saw the darkroom where my prints were developed in the back of the shop. But smells from the bottles of chemicals hung in the musty air. That one-room studio was cool in the winter and hot in the summer, most likely because it was next to impossible to control the temperature in a rambling room with little insulation.

At times a body needed a professional picture made. There were no big chain studios to go to, but a few doors farther down East Magnolia was Jackson's Photo where Pierce Jackson took clear, crisp pictures with his old-fashioned, clumsy cameras. Long-necked lamps stood at intervals, adjusted at angles to prevent a glare on the still photographs of girls announcing up-coming weddings. A bay window displayed bridal portraits and birthday pictures. But for the most part, folks loaded a camera with a roll of film and took their own pictures.

I've never had a camera I liked as much as my first Brownie box camera. It was like a magic thing to me. I'd drop a roll of 110 film into the innards of the fixed-focus camera, wind the film advance around, hold the black box about waist high, gaze into the view finder, and start shooting. I never understood the first thing about shutter speed, focusing, mirrors, or light. All I knew was point and shoot.

These days while others are tossing out their state of the arts cameras in favor of the digital kind, I'm hounding flea markets in search of an old Kodak box camera.

Dime Store Days

When it comes to possessions, I'm 100 percent American. Why in the world are we all so fond of our stuff? Whenever something gets broken, chipped, torn, worn out, or lost, I tend to grieve. Whether it's an old coffee cup or a dog-eared paperback.

Once I left an Auburn sweatshirt at a North Georgia mountain lodge, and I still get depressed when I think about it. It wasn't expensive, and I could've easily replaced it. The fact that I still wish I hadn't left it is sad.

I didn't grow up in the Depression era. And I wasn't around for World War II. I know the biblical verses about laying up treasures in heaven instead of on earth. So why am I so concerned about worldly goods?

I think it all started with five-and-dime stores. You can hardly find a dime store anymore. Fact is, they're so rare that even the name sounds funny.

I ran into a friend in the middle of a mega-store. "Remember the old dime stores?" she asked me.

I sighed. "We called them ten-cent stores."

We swapped stories, walking down the aisles of our memories, picking up puzzles, stamp-pads, pocketknives, and paddles with little rubber balls attached to rubber band strings. The dime store had been an important part of both of our small-town lives.

Auburn was big enough in the 1950s to have two dime stores. Crest 5 & 10 on East Magnolia Avenue and V.J. Elmore 5 & 10 on North College Street. Of all the stores in downtown Auburn, Crest was the most appealing to a kid. Mr. Berman, the owner, welcomed browsers—even young children. We had our pennies for bubble gum and nickels for candy. We walked and looked, picked up and pondered. And sometimes we bought.

Toys were in the back, near the McCall's and Simplicity pattern books, zippers, pincushions, packets of straight-pins in neat pierced rows, and bolts of fabric. While mothers perched on high stools searching for the perfect pattern, children caressed the latest fashions in doll clothes, rubber snakes, colored clay and cap-guns.

We marched up and down the aisles like men with a mission. Even school supplies seemed special on dime store shelves. Mounds of multicolored construction paper, Scotch tape, paper clips, and yellow number-two pencils.

Sturdy pots and pans, can openers and paring knives lay across the aisle from frivolous party supplies. Brightly colored paper cups and plates, candles and sugary cake decorations.

Little girls covetously eyed the cosmetics. A row of shelves filled with the paraphernalia of beauty. Maybelline mascara, Cover Girl compacts, and raunchy-red lipstick. And there were exotic scents like Chantilly and Evening in Paris.

I longed to explore the mysterious bowels of the back room where Mr. Berman sometimes disappeared to search through unpacked boxes. But I never got the chance. At 8:13 on Sunday morning January 15, 1979, a gas leak touched off an explosion that blew away buildings in downtown Auburn. The blast, known far and wide as the Great Kopper Kettle Catastrophe, also destroyed Crest 5 & 10.

For years Auburn folks have mourned the loss of the Kopper Kettle. I wouldn't mind scarfing down another piece of the Kettle's coconut cream pie. But mostly I bemoan the end of an era. The Dime Store Days.

Green Stamps

Whatever happened to Green Stamps? Most young people these days don't have a clue what us older folks are talking about when we mention the tiny green stamps we once hated to lick.

Looking back I recall the days of grocery shopping and that added bonus of getting S&H Green Stamps at the checkout counter. The more groceries you bought, the more stamps you were given. Eventually you saved up enough stamps to drive to the redemption center in Columbus, Georgia and trade them for merchandise.

No kidding. You could get pretty much whatever you wanted with Green Stamps—from blenders to life insurance policies. Thumbing through the catalog was better than poring over the Sears & Roebuck Wish Book. Page after page of goods all for the price of a sore tongue.

Not everything was listed in the catalog, but you could negotiate with the company for almost anything. A school in Erie, Pennsylvania saved up 5.4 million Green Stamps and bought a pair of gorillas for the local zoo.

My mother used Green Stamps to get a set of china for our family in the late 1950s. She said she'd let me pick the pattern if I would lick the stamps and put them in the book. So I did, and I chose white dishes with pink dogwood blossoms.

Years later I used Green Stamps to get a Coleman lantern and stove and a luggage rack for my VW Bug. Friends and relatives pitched in some of their stamps to help me get that gear in time for a camping trip to California.

Inside the redemption center, gripping the worn stamp books with sweaty hands, I was always tempted to change my mind about the merchandise. Rows of sparkling kitchenware would catch my eye, competing with colorful bedspreads, games, electrical equipment, and patio furniture. Stuff I wanted. Things I needed. And I had the wherewithal—in the form of stamps—to acquire them. In those pre-credit card days, my greed took a different form.

There were other brands of colored stamps created by different companies—Top Value, Yellow, Plaid, and Shur-Valu are some I recall. But Sperry & Hutchinson, distributor of S&H Green Stamps, was the most popular of all the competing stamp companies.

When the program reached its peak in the mid-1960s, Sperry and Hutchinson was printing three times as many stamps as the U.S. Postal Service and its catalog may have been the largest single publications in the country.

After the 1970's recession hit, stamps programs diminished, then faded away. Sperry and Hutchinson was sold in 1981 by the founders' offspring.

But a member of the founding Sperry family bought it back from a holding firm in 1999. At that time, there were still about 100 stores offering Green Stamps.

If you have boxes of Green Stamps hidden away in your attic, there's good news. You can still trade them in for either cash or merchandise. Cash value of 1,200 stamps is $1.20. And you can get a catalog by calling 1-800-435-5674.

The company has rebounded with the birth of the Internet. Now it offers "greenpoints" as rewards for online purchases. Check it out at http://www.greenpoints.com. It's true. Green Stamps are still around. But like everything else they've gone virtual. Now I suppose you have to lick your monitor.

I wonder if I can get a new blender?

Lead Pencil

The iceman cometh. And goeth. Along with the milkman, the blacksmith, and the buffalo soldier.

While some occupations have vanished, others have sprung up. And some jobs have been replaced by machines. There's no way around it. Change is as certain as death and taxation.

Historically, there have been those who opposed change. The Luddites, a group of early 19th century English workmen, attempted to prevent the use of laborsaving machinery by destroying it. Fearing they would be replaced by technology, the Luddites rioted against textile machines.

A similar non-violent group started in 1992. The Lead Pencil Club is a worldwide organization with members from San Francisco and New York to India and Austria. Bill Henderson, editor of Pushcart Press and a charter member of the club says, "Tools shouldn't replace important items." He insists, "You can't write better on a word processor. The name indicates words are being processed. How do you process words?"

I have to agree. If we assume a person writes better on a word processor, we have to suppose that the words of Faulkner, Welty, and Steinbeck weren't up to snuff. And what about Shakespeare, Cervantes, and Dickens? Not to mention Tolstoy or Austen.

Before the invention of the typewriter in 1868, writers had to crank out their words with quills, pens, or pencils. After the patent of the Remington, the typewriter reigned for about a hundred years.

Now it seems the typewriter, overthrown by computers, has all but disappeared. Names like Smith-Corona and Royal are about as extinct as Pterodactyls. Most modern writers have switched to computers, but some remain faithful to traditional methods. David McCullough pecks out his biographies on an ancient upright Underwood typewriter. And Anne Tyler churns out award-winning novels with a fountain pen, while others refuse to give up sharp yellow pencils and legal pads.

In *Life on the Mississippi* Mark Twain betrayed certain ambivalent attitudes he had about technology. He distrusted the machines that were transforming his world. At the same time, he greatly admired them. My feelings exactly.

I typed the first short story I sold on a manual Remington typewriter. Later I switched to an IBM electric model. I still have the Remington, and it's hard to believe I was able to type a legible manuscript on it. Like most writers, I've sold out. I prefer the feel and the sound of a typewriter. But punching out words on the computer is easier.

The desk in my study is long—the length of the wall. In the center is my HP computer. To the left is the IBM Selectric covered with reference books and dust, and to the right is the manual. One day a certain wide-eyed 6-year-old pointed to the Remington. "Can I type on it?" she blurted out. "I've never seen a computer like that."

Love is Blind

You may have heard it said that love is blind. Well, I'm here to tell you it's true. This revelation hit me not long ago when I found a skilled worker who was able to get my 1975 MG Midget up and running. Don't get me wrong. It wasn't the mechanic that set my heart fluttering. The thing I noticed was that I absolutely adore that little car.

It all started years ago when I passed the tiny convertible twice a day taking my daughter to school. The "For Sale" sign on the windscreen caught my attention every single time. So after two weeks of looking and longing, it was mine.

Fifteen years have passed, and I've had my share of adventures that a lesser woman wouldn't have put up with. There were the times I got caught in cascading rains, and the wipers wouldn't budge. And the morning I was running late to teach in the Haley Center. The engine died at the Foy Union Building, a good fourth-mile from the parking lot. I shoved it into neutral and started to coast. I figured if the light at the bottom of the hill didn't turn red, I might make it. Racing through the light, I picked up enough speed to turn into the lot and down that last incline to my parking spot.

I've gotten some of my best praying done while driving that shrewish sports car, and over the years, I've become friendly with such foreign terms as "hydraulic clutch," "starter solenoid" and "fly wheel." But there aren't many things more beautiful than a British racing green MG Midget—the graceful lines as sleek as a galloping racehorse or a sloop on a broad reach. So now, it's been repaired again. And of course, it still has a few problems. For instance, the window on the driver's side rolls to the rhythm of an out-of-step soldier. If it's rained the night before and the outside temperature is between 70 and 76 degrees, the window cranks down smoothly all the way. Unfortunately, this same set of conditions causes a noise under the bonnet that would make you swear tree frogs have nested. Or it might just make you swear.

On days that are sunny and cool, the window turns down halfway if you apply pressure to the glass with your left hand while twisting the handle with your right. This wouldn't be such a problem if the turn indicator worked. But because it doesn't, I drive with the window down even on icy mornings and hope drivers understand arm signals. The gas gauge doesn't work either, but the odometer does, so I keep track of the mileage for the 7-gallon tank.

Lately I've noticed a teal green Kharman Ghia with a white ragtop scooting around town. When I spot it, my breathing slows and I get a bit swimmy-headed. Is it greed? Covetousness? Infatuation? Some might call me a fickle two-timer. All I can say is, it seems I have plenty of love to go around.

On the Road

"The world is a book, and those who
do not travel read only one page."

St. Augustine

Atlanta

Atlanta was intriguing to me when I was young, and I've had a soft spot for the place ever since. It was long ago in the late 1960s. I'd just graduated from Auburn and was taking graduate courses at Emory and Georgia State.

I moved from one furnished apartment to the next, all in the northeast section of the city. There was an elegant upstairs efficiency apartment in a white-columned home on Ponce de Leon Avenue and a two-room attic apartment on Fairview Road. Then I got a dog, and I moved to a not so nice place on Dekalb Avenue where I stayed until I ended up back on Ponce de Leon. When I took Frodo, the tri-colored fuzzy faced mutt, to walk I'd make a circle passing the two upstairs apartments where I'd lived before.

The small mint-green house was within walking distance of most places I wanted to go. First thing in the morning I'd traipse a half-mile up the cracked sidewalk to Plaza Drugstore for my daily *Atlanta Constitution*. And there was a little branch library and used-book store nearby.

Fifty yards from my doorstep I caught the bus downtown to Georgia State College. We called it LSU for Luckie Street University. I was such a small-town girl that every bus ride dazzled me. I'd hunker down breathing in exhaust fumes as the bus groaned and sighed along Piedmont Rd., Peachtree St., Spring St., and Auburn Ave. And wide-eyed, I tried to absorb every scene, like a human camcorder. A steep-spired church resembling a gingerbread house, the blue-topped Regency Hyatt House, and the gold-domed Capitol. Pony-tailed and bearded boys and young girls with frizzy hair and clunky shoes marching from Five Points to the white citadel of learning a block away.

I drove the couple of miles from my house to Emory University. A pastoral drive along dogwood-dappled roads to a sprawled out, stately campus. Then I'd rush to class through a medley of azaleas, camellias, and ginkgo trees waving me on with their fan-shaped leaves.

Nights and weekends were cornucopias overflowing with an abundance of pleasing possibilities. I could swim at Piedmont Park or walk at the zoo; sip Espresso at a coffeehouse or scarf down a Varsity chilidog; enjoy a lively Braves' game, or escape to the relative calm of the Cyclorama, the Fox Theater or the High Museum of Art.

I never missed the lighting of the gigantic Christmas tree atop the downtown Rich's Department Store the first Saturday in December. Squashed among a mass of rapt humanity I could never hold back an ecstatic "ahhh" the instant the lights burst into flame. At that precise moment, the Christmas season began for me, and was followed by weeks of frantic shopping, mostly at that same multi-level Rich's store which preceded today's malls, but was almost a mall itself.

Of course this was before Jimmy Carter was President, before Ted Turner and cable television, when the Braves were my team not America's team, before the Olympics, and before the interstate highway looked like a gnarled pretzel.

Still the thought of renting a tiny furnished apartment in the northeast section of the city again is enormously appealing. I haven't done it yet, but I might. I'll report back.

Beach Life

Life at the beach is different from life at home. It's a more simple way of existing, less worldly than life in town. At the coast, like a prisoner shedding his shackles, I feel myself shake off the worries I carry around every day.

I could tell a difference even when I was a little girl. Mama, Daddy, Jane and I took a yearly trip to the Gulf of Mexico in May, a rite of spring, a passage into summer. We'd pile in the car and crank down the windows, letting the wind doing its best to cool us off.

The excitement built until a whiff of salty gulf air drifted in, and at last, I'd spy a patch of sugar-white sand. As soon as I got to the familiar cottage, I'd slip out of my shoes and hit the beach.

Decades have passed, and these days I go to the South Carolina coast, but things are much the same. I check into the high-rise hotel, and shoeless, head straight for the warm waves, hopping hurriedly across the burning sand.

I get up much later in the morning than I would at home, but before anybody else is awake. With a cup of coffee in one hand and a plastic Food Lion bag in the other, I walk close to the water, head down, looking for shells. Back home, there's a gaggle of glass containers of various sizes and shapes filled with Myrtle Beach sand and shells. They dot the mantle, the piano, and the dressers. But I can't help myself. I try to be selective, promising myself I'll only pick up the best ones. It's early, so there are still plenty of good shells tempting me. I spot one, pick it up, and rub off the sand with my thumb and forefinger. I'm drawn to its beauty, and poke it in the bag.

The ocean breeze tangles my hair as I listen to the familiar beach sounds. There's the crash of the waves breaking on the shore as the tide comes in, the haunting shrieks of seagulls searching the beach for scraps of food, and the squeak-squeak of wet sand squishing underneath my bare feet.

The beach trips of my youth come to mind—the scorched skin that peeled of in wide strips like gauze, and the sun poisoning. I know now what I didn't know then. Too much sun is bad for my health. I'm glad I remembered to slather on sunscreen and put a tee shirt over my bathing suit.

My beach days are shaped by simple pleasures. Idylls on the balcony, afternoons sitting under one of the red, yellow, or blue umbrellas my sister has rented, and irresistible reading—a British cozy mystery or the latest Fannie Flagg. Confidences exchanged while the waves lap at ankles, laughter, and an abundance of seafood.

I live much of my life in a state William James so aptly described in the German word, "Zerrissenheit—torn-to-pieces-hood." And I wish all my days could be as carefree as times at the beach.

Camp Helen

Every year about this time I start getting stir crazy, and I catch myself saying, "What I need is a trip to the beach." There's a perfectly good reason for my wanderlust. It all started when I was a little girl and my family made an annual pilgrimage to Panama City Beach.

Sometime toward the end of the school year my sister Jane and I would get checked out around noon on Friday. And we'd sit out on the concrete steps of the school building to wait for Mama and Daddy. While everybody else sweated and worked math problems or diagramed sentences, we'd watch for the Ford to turn into the circular driveway, and then we'd be off, windows down, hair blowing, heading for the Gulf of Mexico.

The Alabama Textile Manufacturers Association owned a compound of cabins on the gulf. And once a year the members of the ATMA and their families met at Camp Helen for a weekend getaway.

By late afternoon I could smell the salty gulf-air through the rolled-down windows and spot patches of marshy soil along the shoulder of Highway 98. And soon we'd cross over a little bridge and somebody would yell, "There it is! There's Camp Helen!"

I didn't take time to look around our bungalow. I kicked off my shoes and headed straight for the beach, toe-dancing to avoid sand burrs. I couldn't wait to wade out to a sand bar, jump in the foam of a breaking wave, or watch bobbing boats on the horizon.

Next morning I'd hit the beach as soon as the sun poked out and play until noon. After a lazy lunch, while the grown-ups rested, Jane and I skipped down the dusty road toting buckets, in search of ripe blackberries. And for an hour or so there was the steady cadence of plump berries plunking in the pail. The temptation to pop one in my mouth was outweighed by the thoughts of Mama back home in the kitchen baking a deep-dish blackberry pie.

I could picture her measuring flour and Crisco into a bowl while the sugarcoated blackberries simmered on the stove. She'd roll out the dough till it was as thin as a Magnolia leaf and cut it in inch-wide strips. The warp and woof of those dough-strips on the pie looked like a loosely woven potholder. When the dish came out of the oven, the berries would be bubbling beneath the golden latticework pastry.

While I dreamed of the deep-dish dessert and mechanically plopped berries into the bucket, my skin burned to a nice shade of maroon. I always forgot that the Six-Twelve insect repellent and Coppertone suntan lotion had long since washed off in the warm waves. And I was left with a second-degree burn and splotched with mosquito bites the size of Indian-head nickels.

With brimming buckets we headed back to the clapboard cottage, sunburned legs shuffling up the path, blistered feet crunching the scalding sand. And I'd vow, "Never again!"

Forty-something years later I tend to forget the sun poisoning, the burned skin, and sand in my cold, wet bathing suit. I don't think about the sulfur water that smelled and tasted like rotten eggs.

Instead I recall the cool sea breeze blowing my hair and the waves below my plastic float rocking my cares away. I can almost hear the shrill cries of the seagulls as they dip and soar and the squeak of the soggy sand beneath my toes. There's the slapping of the surf breaking on the shore, and before bedtime children in beach chairs crooning "Tell Me Why The Stars Do Shine" over and over in rounds.

It's no wonder I find myself saying, "What I need is a trip to the beach."

Driving Rain

Walking my dogs in the late afternoon, I spot a gaggle of geese gliding along at a fast pace. Flying in V formation, geese conserve enough energy to give them 71 percent more flight distance than they'd have flying alone. Some Canada Geese fly with relatives, but nobody really knows what impulse drives other migrating birds to join a particular flock. Do they seek out birds they know and trust, or is it random?

As I ponder avian flight patterns, it occurs to me that driving on the interstate might be similar to the camaraderie of soaring migrating geese. Are the birds anonymous strangers brought together on flyways like automobiles meeting on a highway?

I'm known at Chattooga Gym in Marietta, GA as "the one who drives from Alabama every week." When I made the decision last year to commit to my daughter Emily's lessons each Tuesday, I did so with a bit of foolhardy bravado. But for at least six months, I left instructions written on a 3 x 5 card propped between the keys on my computer keyboard revealing the whereabouts of my last-will-and-testament. And before setting out for home at night after practice, I'd chug enough caffeine to rouse the comatose.

Now I don't give it much thought. But driving home on the interstate highways after dark has some dangers. Many nights I'm bombarded by fierce blowing rains. There's a black splotch on the weather map—an oval shaped abyss stretching from Marietta to Auburn.

At times the rain is so thick on I-75 I can't see beyond the headlights. After 7 miles of careful maneuvering, I change to the I-285 bypass, but it's no better. When I turn onto I-85 the rain is blinding. I'm relieved when I come to a truck ahead, and I follow its taillights as best I can as we creep along at thirty miles an hour. A car comes up behind me, followed by another and another. They can't pass. There isn't enough visibility to try. We make a little caravan moving through the black hole. We drive twenty or thirty miles together, and I wonder if they're as grateful for the company and taillights showing the way as I am.

The truck turns off at Newnan, blinking brake lights in good-bye as he exits. I blink my headlights back. Now I'm the leader, going slower without the truck's lights to guide me. Still no one can pass. The car behind me turns off at Lagrange—I'm surprised when that driver, too, blinks his lights when turning off. The rain lets up just past West Point, and we finally speed up to the limit, but the cars behind me don't rev up and pass. We stay in our little migratory flock until, one by one, we reach our destination and blink farewell until at last I take exit 58 to Tiger Town, saying good-bye to Interstate-85.

At the risk of sounding bird brained, it seems I have a lot in common with traveling geese.

Summer Dig

Fast moving, rumble, tumble stagecoaches. They call to mind teams of lathered horses at a dead run, corset-encased ladies delicately dabbing moisture from their brows, Bible-toting preachers dressed in black, and bad-boy gamblers with hidden handguns.

I cut my permanent teeth on western movies that portrayed the era of the stagecoach. Every time the preacher settled down to read his Bible, bandits raced out of the woods in pursuit of the payroll-carrying stagecoach. The driver frantically slapped the reins pushing those horses for all they were worth while the tobacco-chewing sidekick fought them off.

Truth is most people traveled by stagecoach in American frontier days. Travel was slow and uncomfortable. The coaches bumped along night and day, covering about 100 miles in 24 hours. Passengers, grimy with dust in summer and shivering with cold in winter, tried to sleep on the hard seat. Out West crude adobe stations every 10 miles or so provided food for passengers and horses. Back East there were stagecoach inns.

The coming of the steam locomotive changed everything. In 1831 South Carolina began the first regularly scheduled steam-powered train service in the United States. And in no time stagecoaches were gone and with them went the stagecoach inn.

But I spent the summer of 1968 at a stagecoach inn in the foggy foothills of north Georgia. Tumbledown Jarrett Manor on the outskirts of Toccoa, Georgia spread out on a grassy bluff. I was working for the Georgia Historical Commission as part of an archaeological dig.

We spent our first night on the floor of the wooden building that had fallen into a state of disrepair. But the next day we pitched our tents on the lawn and slept there for the rest of the summer. Our bathroom was an old outhouse and we took showers in a makeshift stall in the corner of the shed where artifacts were washed and catalogued. And we cooked our meals on a campfire.

Bill Kelso, the state archaeologist, lived in a tiny turtle of a trailer with his wife and two toddlers. He'd gotten there early with compass and transit, making maps and setting up a grid system with stakes and twine. Neat, precise squares covered with sheets of plastic pockmarked the grounds waiting for us to excavate.

My plan was to get a gorgeous tan on the dig. Instead I spent most of that summer underneath the house with a trowel, a dustpan and a soft, two-inch paint brush sweeping dirt into the pan and at the same time working on a good case of brown lung disease.

We found evidence of Creek Indian occupation, a dry well, a smoke-house, a graveyard, and a kitchen away from the main structure. The stage-coach inn, called Traveler's Rest, was dated in the early 1800s. Inside was a public lobby where stagecoach tickets were sold and rooms could be rented for the night. It was there that the men could smoke and have a few drinks. There was also a ladies' parlor where the women could rest, and a large dining room. Upstairs were rooms for travelers to sleep.

I'm probably one of the few people around who can claim to have slept in an authentic stagecoach inn. When I think of that era, I imagine toothless Gabby Hayes riding shotgun, fighting off Injuns, then stopping at a stagecoach station for a mug of "sassparilly." Then I conjure up visions of rainy nights in a tent listening to Braves' baseball on a transistor radio, ankles covered in redbug bites, early morning dew, and coffee cooked on coals. And I recall the murder mystery I planned to write. It would be set at a dig in North Georgia and called *Trowel and Error*. For me those times seem as long gone as the old stagecoach days.

Trips Across the USA

When the weather turns cold, I like to warm my toes by a wood fire while I visit the back roads I've traveled on sunnier days. Sometimes the memories are a bit blurry, like viewing an impressionist painting from across the room. And as I sort out the pieces of the puzzle, it's the little things I call up.

More often than not, I reminiscence about food, and the scenic wonders of America aren't nearly as vivid as the morsels I've enjoyed. I don't remember the sun-drenched colors of Santa Fe as clearly as I recall eating a baloney sandwich in a parking lot in Albuquerque while my underwear tumbled in the launderette dryer. I've spread ham-sandwich-lunches on a quilt at the Continental Divide, Petrified Forest, and Death Valley.

My history of eating on the road started when I was a little girl. There weren't any fast-food restaurants back then. When we took a trip, Mama made tomato sandwiches and hardboiled eggs before we left home, and we gobbled those lunches wherever we could find a picnic spot.

Since then, I've driven through practically every state in the U.S.A. Most of my travels were camping trips, so I've grown partial to early morning coffee with a few cinders floating on top. Thumbing through an old cookbook the other day I ran across a recipe for Flyaway Pancakes, and I groaned out loud recalling a windy morning in Kansas when my plate of hotcakes was carried off by a gust of wind.

My clearest picture of the Grand Canyon is scarfing down barbecue chicken and corn-on-the-cob with the manners of Henry the Eighth. We pulled into the campground as the sun was setting, and by the time we got the fire going and the chicken on the makeshift grill, we were starving. That half-cooked bird was the best I've ever eaten.

At times when I'm traveling, I'll stop at a restaurant. Any trip west of the Mississippi River becomes a quest for A&W Root Beer. And I make it a point to have a frosty mug of the bubbly drink with two scoops of vanilla ice cream whenever I find an old-timey A&W drive-in.

Following the Lewis and Clark Trail in Idaho, I ate hazelnut toast and Marianberry jam with my over-easy eggs at Down the Street Family Restaurant in Coeur d'Alene, and gulped down a 49-cent hotdog at a Stinker Station Handi-Mart in Payette.

I happily remember eating crawfish in Baton Rouge, Indian fry-bread in Taos, and salmon in Seattle.

Not long ago my daughter Emily asked me, "What did you like best about our trip to Wales?" After careful consideration, I had to admit, "The little restaurant where I had eggs on toast and a pot of tea." Seems my scavenger hunt along back roads has gone international.

Two Kinds of Vacations

There are two kinds of vacations—first class and with children. I vaguely remember the first class kind, but it's been too long to recollect fully. It's that second sort I'm prone to take. Come on. Admit it. Unless you became a cloistered nun at age nineteen, you know exactly what I'm talking about.

Before you hit the interstate you're barraged with age-old questions: "How much farther?" or "Are we there yet?" Then there are the eternal complaints: "She's touching me." "He's looking at me." "She's breathing on me—on purpose." When you've been on the road exactly one hour you hear: "Can we stop and eat?" "I forgot my bathing suit" (If you're headed for the beach.), "I forgot my coat" (If your destination is the far north.), or "I think I left the tackle box in the garage." (If it's a fishing trip.)

And of course, if you're winding around a scenic mountain road with no place to pull over or you're stuck in an inner-city, radiator-boiling traffic jam there are cries of "I've gotta go!" or "I'm gonna throw up!" This is almost unavoidable if you have just purchased a vehicle that still has that new car smell.

I'm not as hale and hearty as some people are. I've never taken several small children at one time on an extended vacation. Somehow I was inherently aware of the axiom, "Never attempt an auto trip if your kids outnumber the car windows." But I understand some folks do it all the time. They pack up the whole clan (including Grandma and Cranky the dog) and go camping in the Alaskan wilderness. Then, when they get back home, they have enough energy left to write a travel article about it. And it always sounds so happy. "What a delightful breakfast it was. As the sun came up, Daddy and Buffy showed up with their daily catch, a string of shining salmon. Five-year-old Teeny had built a roaring fire, and the twins had made a batch of their special Indian fry-bread. Little Frankie, our toddler, crept around the rough-hewn table putting out hand-woven placemats that Grandma had made from indigenous foliage." The mother doesn't seem to have lifted a finger. But, then, she wrote the article that paid for the trip.

My family vacations have been more ordinary—long, hot trips to the beach. The first time I took the children to the gulf, I was so naïve that I actually packed a copy of *Anna Karenina*. My plan was to loll on a beach blanket and improve my mind while the children frolicked in the sand. That was my idea. Their idea was to cover me with sand, wet seaweed, and salt water and show me twenty-five broken sea shells, one sand dollar, three dead crabs, a Popsicle stick, an enormous sand castle they had built, ten cigarette butts, and a little boy whose bathing trunks had fallen off. For the record, don't think I didn't get any reading done. I just had to select my material more carefully. *Anna Karenina* was out, but we read a whole collection of Little Golden Books, including *Little Peewee* and *Busy Timmy*.

Many of these trips were disasters as far as rest and relaxation were concerned, but while I was definitely daunted, I was never willing to give up. (Remember F. Scott Fitzgerald got 120 rejections before *This Side of Paradise* was accepted for publication.)

I've made mistakes with my family's vacations. I'll be the second to admit it. These bloopers will probably be made clear when my children decide to write columns of their own. But I do learn from my blunders. And this is my strategy for family road trips. Wait until the youngest child is twenty-one and no longer spills milk, gets knots in his shoelaces, or puts pebbles in his nose. And if you feel compelled to take young children along in the car, don't go any farther than the mailbox on the corner.

Wanderlust

When I glance back a couple of years, it seems I was suffering from severe wanderlust. I'd tell friends that I yearned to take a trip and they'd ask, "Where do you want to go?" That was part of the problem. There wasn't just one place I was dying to visit. I had a ton of trips I longed to take. I collected magazines with tempting pictures of European villas. I hoarded *Reader's Digest* volumes on traveling back roads of the U.S. I googled MapQuest plane, train, and automobile destinations. And I had dreams of becoming a travel writer, even though I could barely make it to the Loachapoka Syrup Sopping.

But that was before I took my first trip with my daughter Emily's Special Olympics rhythmic gymnastics team. I hardly knew Cindy Bickman, the team coach, at the time. Emily and I were at the gym in Marietta, GA, about to head out the door to drive back to Auburn, when I overheard Cindy talking about trips to Greece and England with some special needs athletes. Standing there with my mouth slightly ajar, with the expression of a spoiled four-year-old, I blurted out, "I wanna go!" And for once, my big mouth actually paid off. I thought I was kidding around, but she said, "You can't go to Greece. We've already been. But you can go to England." I went back to my mouth-open pose, but Cindy kept talking. "It's late so you'll have to let me know soon." I had five minutes to consult Emily and give Cindy an answer. Back then, Emily was a homebody. But, without much thought, she grinned and said, "Yes!"

So two months later I was on a Delta flight to England with 12 Special Olympic rhythmic gymnasts, 5 teenage helpers, 2 coaches and some Mamas and Papas. Our mission was a therapeutic competition with a British disabilities team, but it turned into a whirlwind of fun for a week all over England and Wales.

Then twelve months later fifty-two of us from Chattooga flew to Switzerland. Our goal was to perform at the 14th World Gymnaestrada in Lausanne. There were ten days of non-stop adventure, including hiking in the Alps and a boat ride across Lake Geneva to Evian, France for dinner.

As it turned out, for me, wanderlust is not something that can be satisfied by wandering. Just like eating one donut revs up my craving for sugar and fat, each trip makes me crazy for another. It's barely November, and I'm already restless.

But at least now I know where I want to go. Explorers call it true north. For me true north is wherever the Chattooga group goes. There's nobody else I'd want to travel with. And the truth is, if I overhear Cindy say, "We're going to a Guantanamo Bay this summer," I'll assume my pampered-four-year-old stance and blurt out, "I wanna go!"

Back in the Day

"Memory is the diary we carry
around with us."

Oscar Wilde

Aprons

The phone rang. Stirring a pot of sticky split-pea soup with one hand, I grabbed the receiver with the other. Somewhere in the process of mixing and talking I noticed a blob of bile green liquid trickling down my favorite shirt. In a nook between the refrigerator and cupboard an assortment of aprons hung forgotten and unused.

Nowadays only a few dedicated cooks spend much time standing over their self-cleaning ovens. And when we do cook, we dress in jeans and t-shirts. So why bother with an apron?

In my mother's day there was good reason to wear aprons. In those blissful pre-cholesterol times foods were fried in bacon grease, spitting hot fat far and wide. Thick strips of dough were dropped into a pot of boiling broth to make dumplings. And baking a cake was a long and loving process of mixing flour and eggs and sugar and butter.

So Mama always wore an apron when she cooked. She had a variety to pick and choose from among the bright displays on hooks in the broom closet. Ruffled aprons, striped aprons, old-fashioned checkered aprons trimmed with rickrack, and cross-stitched gift aprons.

No blue jeans or sweat pants for the women of that generation. They wore plain, functional housedresses for cooking and cleaning, and those who didn't were thought to be strange. Mama wore a sturdy apron over her dress for extra protection. She tied it around her middle in the morning and kept it there most of the day.

Sometimes Mama chose a fresh apron for cooking supper, a large one with a bib that hung around her neck and roomy pockets that held handkerchiefs or recipes. But if company was coming, she'd pick a frilly, dainty one.

Mama's aprons were as much a part of her as her blue-gray eyes, the sweet smelling lotions she used, and the songs she sang while she worked. When I was sick, she'd climb the stairs after breakfast with her apron still tied around her waist. Reading the Eleanor Estes' *Moffat* books aloud to me, she would laugh so hard tears streamed down her face, and she'd use the hem of her apron to wipe her eyes. Those aprons, like Mama, were tough but soft, practical and pretty.

As the youngest child in our family I lolled in the kitchen watching my mother cook while my older siblings went about more important business. And when Mama turned her back, I'd sneak up behind her pulling one end of the neat apron bow, untying it, so I could hear her say, "Aw-Pshaw." And I was amazed at the way she re-tied a perfect bow behind her back without looking.

Like other Baby Boomers, I never acquired the habit of wrapping an apron around my waist. Somehow I feel silly covering up cut-off jeans. It's only after a lump of spaghetti sauce has bubbled up and popped out of the pan onto my clothes that I look longingly at the untouched aprons hanging limply and accusingly on the wall.

Most children these days have never rushed in from school to find their mother wearing an apron. Fact is, one thing we can't say about the youth of today is that they're tied to their mother's apron strings.

Drive-in Movies

What ever happened to drive-in movies? For that matter, who even remembers them? A twelve-year-old girl interviewed on a television newscast said well of course she knew what a drive-in movie was. "You sit outside in lawn chairs and watch a big-screen TV."

As a little girl there was nothing I liked more than jumping in the car and heading for an outdoor picture show. My love affair with drive-ins started when all my baby teeth were still intact. Daddy bought a parcel of land on the river and built a rock cabin for a family getaway. He taught me to mix cement when I was five years old, my sister Jane and I working together mixing half a bag at a time. And our pay was an occasional trip to the local Langdale Drive-In. It was our daily lunchtime ritual to climb the hill to my Aunt Mary's house and search her *Valley Daily Times News* hoping to find that a good movie was playing that night.

It was worth any amount of weekly work for a couple of hours at the drive-in. At half-past sundown, we'd pile in the car and drive down the blacktop road to the theater. Then we'd pick a spot to our liking and hook the speaker to a rolled down window. When the movie started, Jane and I sat spellbound watching the new "Ma and Pa Kettle" or "Francis the Talking Mule" while Daddy's shoulders slumped as he dozed and slapped at mosquitoes.

Later as a teenager in Auburn, I spent lots of Friday and Saturday nights at the Auburn-Opelika Drive-In on Opelika Road. We'd stuff as many bodies as we could fit in somebody's daddy's car and head for an outside movie. The pictures we liked to watch at the drive-in were the scary ones like "The Blob" or "The Incredible Shrinking Man." I have a memory that comes sneaking up when I'm not thinking of anything in particular and catches me by surprise. We're at the drive-in, my adolescent friends and I. It's one of those hot muggy nights and we're sharing bags of salty popcorn and drinking RC Cola from sweating paper cups. Truth be told it's the camaraderie of the teenage sisterhood more than the movies that sticks in my mind.

When I was a young married student my husband and I would drive back to the Langdale Drive-In on weekend nights. We'd swap our VW bug for Aunt Mary's roomier '54 Ford and spend an evening enjoying the latest comedy. And later when our daughter was a toddler, we'd bundle her up and put her to sleep in the back of our VW Camper while we watched a good detective story.

The drive-in movie industry boomed in the '50s and '60s. But these days drive-in theaters are on the endangered list with whooping cranes and red pandas. From 4,000 screens nationwide in 1958, the number of drive-ins has now dwindled to about 400. They declined with suburban sprawl and with the advent of videotapes.

One of the few I know of is in Jesup, Georgia, south of Savannah. That popular theater draws moviegoers from miles around. The owner bought the theater in 1970 when popcorn was 25 cents and the summer's big hit movie was "Support Your Local Sheriff" starring James Garner. And he's managed to keep the Jesup Drive-In open and thriving. It's an attraction, like Disney World. Lifetime residents of Jesup remember going there with parents as children and taking dates there in high school. Now they take their sons and daughters to the drive-in.

I wish I could load my van with a gaggle of 21st Century children and take them to a drive-in movie. They have no idea what it's like. Pulling into a spot and attaching the speaker to your front window. Munching Milk Duds and guzzling Coca Cola through a straw. Big kids reading the credits to the younger one. Whole families sitting transported in a theater under the stars.

Filling Stations

It's unceasingly sad to see a good business forced to close down. It happens all the time, and we grumble and look around to see whose fault it is. I have a funny feeling we're looking in all the wrong places. Thing is, it's probably our fault.

On the national scene *Life* and the *Saturday Evening Post* were run out of business while the magazine stands are filled with trash. And good newspapers are having a hard time surviving when tabloids are multiplying like maggots.

Locally we've witnessed the demise of every small drugstore. Markle's and Lipscomb's closed their doors, Toomer's turned into a souvenir shop, and Glendean Drugs was replaced by a big chain drugstore.

Unable to compete with mega-stores, honest little hardware stores have rolled over and died. And as we yell, "Quality not quantity" we march into super-stores to buy cheaper goods made in sweat shops.

Family restaurants have hung up "Going out of Business" signs. But one of the saddest changes is the recent departure of locally owned service stations.

When I was a little girl there were filling stations on every corner of downtown Auburn and a few in between. They seemed almost mystical to me. Daddy would pull the Ford into Ingram's Gulf Oil Station on the corner of North Gay Street and Glenn Avenue, park close to the gas pump, and roll the window down. "Fill 'er up," he'd say, and that's when the magic began.

I thought those boys who pumped gas must be geniuses. With just a flick of the wrist they'd turn a lever and shove the nozzle into the gas tank. Somehow they kept the gas flowing while they told Daddy to "pop the hood" and mystically inspected the oil and water. While they checked the air in the tires, the gas cut off by itself.

But the thing that fascinated me most of all was how they washed the windshield. Those boys would slosh soapy water on the dead-bug-and-pollen-covered glass, scrub it with a long-handled rubbery contraption, and scrape it clean. I've never been so entranced by anything in my life.

Sometimes I went inside the dimly lit little office with Daddy to pay. The counter was crowded with a cash register, adding machine, receipt book, bathroom keys on long wooden sticks and a telephone. There was a calendar on the wall and a map stand with free road maps by the door.

Next to the office was the garage where cars were fixed. On a good day I could see a car going up on the rack.

Over the years I discovered that all gas station offices were pretty much alike. Tiny holes in the wall that smelled of oil and gas and dirty rags. And to enter into one was like going into the inner-sanctum of a male ceremonial chamber.

I could've cried when those service stations were torn down one by one. Gas stations have been replaced by mini-marts with do-it-yourself gas pumps. Inside the lights are as bright as Jordan-Hare Stadium, and they're cleaner than some hospital rooms I've seen. You can't buy a quart of oil, but if it's donuts or Cappuccino you need, you're in luck.

It's our own fault. Somewhere, somehow, we went wrong.

Grocery Stores

On a hot August day a few years back, my mother and I were behind two barefoot boys in the express checkout lane at Kroger. Each boy stood maybe four feet high and weighed about as much as a bushel of potatoes. One had skin the color of Godiva chocolate. The other was blond and blue-eyed. One boy held a mountain of change, mostly pennies, in his cupped hands, and together they counted and whispered with their heads almost touching, conferring on their high finances.

Nobody hurried them or got impatient. Mama even offered to float 'em a loan. But they shook their heads and kept counting until at last they were sure they'd come up with $6.42. By that time the front of the fast-paced supermarket had almost come to a halt as shoppers and cashiers watched and smiled, probably trying to remember being that young and determined.

"That could only happen in the South," Mama said. And she was one who knew. She'd been born and bred in Barbour County, Alabama where her father owned J.W.T. Corbitt's General Merchandise Store at the turn of the 20th century. He sold groceries and produce, dry goods, notions and clothing. Flethcer's Castoria, Old Dutch Cleanser, Prince Albert, and Magic Stock Tonic (the best animal regulator).

In those days you told a clerk what you wanted and he brought it to you. No standing in line with ten people in front of you trying to find a coupon or paying with food stamps, credit cards or checks that need approval.

That store burned down long before I was born. But I have dim memories of grocery stores from my 1950's childhood. There was an A&P, a Piggly Wiggly and John Waller's family-run store on the north side of downtown Auburn. And sometime later a Kwik Chek opened up.

At the other end of town was Southside Grocery. To shop there, all you had to do was pick up the phone and call in your order. They'd send a delivery boy to your back door, and you'd get a bill at the end of the month.

As I passed from pigtails to ponytails to big pink rollers and Dippedy-Doo, grocery stores evolved right along with me. In the '50s milk came in glass bottles and butchers cut your meat. Dishwashing powders came in boxes. There was Duz and Dreft, and new blue Cheer. For whiter teeth you could buy Ipana and Chlorodent Toothpaste or Colgate Tooth Powder. And for shinier hair there was Halo, Dreme, and Lustre-Creme Shampoo.

You could buy 5-cent packs of Kool-Aid and six-ounce bottles of Coke. Almost as good as drinking a cold green-bottled Coca-Cola, was looking on the bottom to see what city it came from and whose bottle was from the farthest place. And you could take the empties back and swap them for a penny apiece.

In the '60s, diet drinks like Tab and Fresca were the craze along with TV dinners and instant potatoes. And to entice shoppers, stores began giving savings stamps. Stores became bigger and brighter with more and more items on the shelves.

Truth is, I never thought a whole lot about shopping until I got married. I went straight from floating down the church aisle to wrestling ornery shopping carts down supermarket aisles. Those contrary carts squeak and balk and act up like they have minds of their own, going every which way but my way. Why just last week I touched a display table with the corner of my out-of-control buggy and boxes of lemons flew helter-skelter across the floor of the produce section.

I wish just once I could pick up the phone and call Southside Grocery.

Hanging Clothes

Pleasant days send me outside like a caterpillar busting out of her co-coon, to flit about in the great outdoors. I go from my own backyard to secluded hiking trails where I can sniff wild honeysuckle and listen to happy Mockingbird songs.

On a summer morning in the pavilion at Hickory Dickory Park, I watched a young mother casually pull a soggy Pamper off a bare bottom and toss it in the trash.

"How much do you spend a month on those things?" another mom asks. And a heated discussion erupted on the cost of throwaway diapers.

"I used cloth diapers on my three," I volunteered.

The eyes of the young mothers turned on me as if I'd confessed to offer-ing up my babies as sacrifices to Bacchus. I eased away to a solitary bench and sat alone contemplating past days.

"You bunch of sissies," I felt like hollering. "My mother raised five chil-dren without a washer or dryer, much less plastic pants." But those young women looked worn out in spite of their modern Velcro world, so I kept my thoughts to myself.

When I was small, most women had never laid eyes on a clothes dryer. Back then every house had a clothesline stretched taut in the backyard. I re-member Mama toting heavy baskets of wash outside, shaking out shirts, and pinning pillowcases to the line while wet underwear flapped in the breeze.

As I sat on that hard seat, long-forgotten memories stirred, images of Mama and me hanging clothes and talking. She did the draping while I came behind with a canvas bag of clothespins. She'd reach into my pouch for a wooden pin, hook a dress to the line, and we'd move along to an empty spot of twine, like tightrope walkers beneath the wire.

On breezy, blue-sky days it didn't take long for the sun to soak up the moisture. While I helped Mama fold a double-bed sheet—in half, in fourths, in eighths, down to the size of a throw pillow—I breathed in the scent of sun-dried linen, an aroma that can't be reproduced in a spray can.

On cloudy days, we watched for signs of rain as diligently as Hottentots hunting animal tracks. At the first hint of mist, we'd rush out with the bas-ket, jerk the waterlogged wash from the line, and dash back inside to drape it over bathroom fixtures.

As we made our way across the yard fastening frocks to the tight-pulled cord, Mama told me how backbreaking this chore had been when she was growing up.

Her own mother had twelve children to keep clean. In those days, they did the washing outside once a week in a big tub. First, they filled the wash-tub with water brought up from the well in buckets, then scrubbed the fabric up and down along the humps of a washboard. Wash-water splashed from one side of the tub to the other, sloshing over the sides. Finally, they wrung out the material by hand, and hung the sopping-wet cloth over a long rope strung between two trees.

As I left the park, I strolled past the young mothers and their fancy bags crammed with disposable diapers. I thought about my grandmother, and without turning my head I said, "You go girls."

House on North College Street

North College was the main street in town during the 1950s. And right on the corner of North College and Mitcham Avenue was the big white house where my family lived. I thought that white house was the best house in the whole block to be living in, because it was right in the middle of everything.

If I stood in the very corner of the front yard, I could see all the way down Mitcham. So when Mama went to the A & P to buy groceries, I could see her till she turned onto Gay Street. When she went in the other direction to pick up Daddy's suits at Young's Laundry, I could watch her until the top of her head disappeared down the steep slope. When a tuft of her hair reappeared, I'd cross the street and run to meet her.

Our house was on U.S. Highway 29. I'd stand at the kitchen sink and watch the Greyhound buses from the window. They'd glide by from Atlanta heading to New Orleans, groaning as they shifted gears, stopping at the corner stop sign.

Across the street, the train depot took up the whole block in front of the railroad tracks. My sister Jane and I liked to count the cars on the long freight trains as they clumped along, hoping to get to a hundred. We waved at the people on the passenger trains and the man riding the caboose, and they waved back.

Next door on the other side of College Street, the red brick Sigma Alpha Epsilon fraternity house was a hub of activity. I'd watch the boys come and go, lively and loud. Sometimes they'd cross the street to play catch with Jane and me. In their front yard, the big white lion mascot was a target of other fraternities. And, first thing every morning before heading downstairs for breakfast, I'd glance out the bay window to see if the lion had been painted red or blue.

In our backyard was an old barn with a hayloft. The loft was a hideaway where Jane and I plotted, planned and played. Back then parents didn't worry about rickety ladders, broken floorboards, or open second-story windows.

The house had big rooms with high ceilings. The long, curved railing along the staircase was perfect for sliding down, and nobody ever seemed to mind me coming down that way. Most nights after supper, I'd spend time on the screened-in-porch tossing a baseball at the brick wall and snagging it in my catcher's mitt. There was just one bathroom for our family of seven, but we never thought it was a problem.

After we'd lived there six years, almost half my life, the owner decided to go up on the rent. Daddy said $125 a month was too much, so we built a new house on Cary Drive.

It broke my heart. And now, all these years later, I still miss that house on North College Street.

Porches

In the days of my growing up, before every home had a television set, most houses had a porch or two. They were gathering places where folks sat to talk, snap green beans and shell field peas. Neighbors strolling along the sidewalk would stop and speak. There was an unwritten rule that the passer-by shouldn't join the porch-sitters without an invitation, and conversations were limited to such things as "How's your mother?" and "Is it hot enough for you?"

The family porch brings back a slew of memories from the miry mist of my past. The first porch I recall was the wrap-around kind. It hooked onto the front of my family's white, square house in Georgia. In the late afternoon I'd perch on the top step and wait for my daddy to come home from work. But mostly I claimed the long, broad territory as my personal playground. The banister was just the right height to serve as a bar like the ones I saw the bad guys use in Western movies. Tiny pimento glasses filled with sweet-tea made perfect shot-glasses of whiskey. These were my pre-school days, an ominous start to my future.

When we moved to Auburn, the two-story house on North College Street had a big screened-in porch on the side. I'd given up drinking jiggers of pretend bourbon by the time I was seven, and I switched to tossing a baseball at the porch's brick chimney on rainy days. Later I used the area as a practice room, burping out the low notes to "Aura Lee," moving the slick trombone slide up and down—c, f, e-flat, f, g, d, g.

Aunt Mary's back porch is the one I remember best. The slab of concrete that jutted out from the rear of her clapboard house in Langdale wasn't much to look at. But I believe if I were granted one wish, it would be to go back to that porch on a summer evening after supper. Gardenia bushes in full bloom hugged the house, their sweet smell floating to high heaven. Aunt Mary leaned back on her faded-green chaise-lounge, and roared her booming laugh. I'd come out the screen door and she'd yell, "Don't slam the door," too late. Sometimes we made hand-churned ice cream, but more often Mama's sisters dished store-bought lemon ice-milk from a carton. We ate out of big blue cut-glass bowls and drank tall glasses of Fresca.

The grown-ups talked over the groaning of a plug-in fan as it strained back and forth stirring up the sticky air, keeping flying insects at bay. And children ran helter-skelter with Mason jars on a mission to capture lightning bugs.

In the 1960s ranch-style houses became popular; long one-story dwellings without porches. Central air-conditioning was standard and folks preferred staying inside where it was cool and mosquito-free. Watching television after supper was the norm, and instead of porches, there were patios for family cookouts.

Nowadays the suburban set has switched to decks. What were once porches have been glassed in as sunrooms. We imprison ourselves in bug-free rooms, substituting 70-degree air for friendly faces.

The thing I miss most about porches is there's no good place to sneak off alone when my feelings get hurt. Nowhere to swing in a glider and pout.

Walking Home

I've always felt sorry for children who miss the experience of walking home from school.

My daddy's sagas of his own barefoot walks became more treacherous and unbelievable with each telling. He claimed to have fended off snakes in the hot weather, but his most unlikely tales were of winter walks over icy roads, breaking off ice-layers with his bare toes. The fact that he lived in the little town of Texasville in southernmost Alabama made his yarns improbable.

His early 1900's childhood was not at all like my halcyon days. When I was a small town Auburn girl, we were a one-Ford family. Daddy dropped us off in the morning, but when the bell rang dismissing school for the day, I trudged with my sisters the mile-and- two-tenths home.

Being set free after sitting silent for seven classroom hours was glorious. We talked and laughed almost giddy now that we were finally unfettered. I don't recall how tired and sweaty we must have been in the spring or how cold in the winter. I don't remember feet dragging. I see our playfully hiking 1950's group through a rose colored prism, a Norman Rockwell painting.

I knew every crack in the sidewalks, every chink of uneven pavement. I didn't have to look down to avoid stumping my toe.

Back then the big brick school on Samford Avenue housed grades one through twelve. As soon as the final bell rang I met my sisters Beth and Jane out front and we'd start out like a happy group of refugees heading home from a POW camp. Beth's boyfriend Wayne came along pushing his bicycle. Wayne was the quarterback of the undefeated Auburn High School football team. His teammates joining in the trek seriously impressed my second grade psyche.

The threads of the tapestry changed after that first year. Beth and Wayne graduated, leaving Jane and me to form a different kind of gaggle. Now our gang was made up of a flurry of friends our age. The route never changed. We'd head along Samford Avenue, past the mysterious gingerbread house next door, down the hill to the Southside filling station on the corner.

We'd turn north onto Gay Street and stroll past the Methodist Church, a boarding house, old Dr. Thomas' office, the city library, post office, and stately fraternity houses with carefree boys playing football in the yards. There was the Western Auto and Gulf station on the corner of Gay Street and Glenn Avenue. Once we crossed over the railroad tracks and passed John's Cleaners and the Dari-Delite, we were home free. Turning onto Mitcham Avenue by the railway station, we'd wave so long to Martha and Peggy

Mason who lived on down Gay Street past the A&P next to the Chevrolet dealership. Now we'd speed up. We could almost see our house.

At last, we trudged up the back steps into the kitchen where we'd find Mama in her apron fixing our snack, margarine and sugar on white bread.

I'm glad I grew up in a small town where not much happened and we could saunter home without the fear of being shanghaied. I wish that by some magic I could step through that back screen door one more time happily jabbering, "Mama, I'm home."

West Point

Thomas Wolfe said, "You can't go home again." I don't give much thought to going home again, because I live in the town where I did most of my growing up. But my earliest years were spent in West Point, Georgia, a little town, less than 30 miles away.

I drove to West Point a few Saturdays ago to join in the celebration of the Hawkes Library's 90th anniversary. I'd thought I was free from those Georgia roots, but I found fragments still tugged tenaciously when I went back, teasing—almost tormenting me. Those roots went deeper than I thought. This was the place where I began, and most likely much of who I am was formed there.

As I hurried across the Chattahoochee River Bridge, I dreaded the changes I knew I'd find. I slowed, wondering if anything would be the same, and I longed for sameness.

It didn't take long to be hit by staggering changes. I remember walking across the bridge holding my sister Beth's hand. Back then the library was at the end of the bridge on the right, and on the left was the Riviera movie-theater. Years ago a flood damaged the bridge, so they built a new one behind the library. And now the Riviera is gone.

But, as it happened, the little brick dollhouse of a library is just the same. Inside the wooden front doors, I found the same card catalogue and the same long desk where Mrs. Moore, the librarian, sat in her wheel chair. The books still have the signed library cards from the days when I scratched my name in 6-year-old print. I sat in a tiny chair and thumbed through a picture book, and I was unaware for a moment that I'd spent a lifetime somewhere else.

When I left the incredibly fun gathering at the library, I decided to take a pilgrimage further into the past. I drove idly up and down streets looking for my childhood haunts, uniting happy memories with a dull ache. Reading street signs searching for East Sixth Street, I spotted a Methodist church and when I saw the circular brick driveway, I knew it was where my sister Jane taught me to roller skate. I drove on and felt a stab of excitement as I saw the white house with the wraparound front porch. It was like a smaller version of the house I remembered. There was the porch rail where we pretended to drink sarsaparilla, the yard where Jane was the Lone Ranger and I was Tonto, the sidewalk where I rode my tricycle, and the front steps where I sat to wait for my sisters to get home from school. They were all filled with the ghosts of my past.

I drove home in a mood halfway between longing and contentment. The day had been a sentimental journey with plenty of emotions entangled with memories. I was happy to find that after so many years, the roots remain.

Happy Holidays

"A holiday gives one a chance to
look backward and forward, to
reset oneself by an inner compass."

May Sarton

Christmas

I may be dreaming of a white Christmas, but the truth is I've never known one. And chances are, I'll never have one.

I've read other folks' nostalgic accounts of childhood Christmases. They're filled with reports of old fashioned kinds of winters that bring back memories of Christmases past. Seasons of delight ushered in with the first falling snowflakes. Winter sports—ice skating, snow ball battles, building the biggest snowman, racing down hills on lightning fast bobsleds.

But the Christmases I knew as a little girl were much more likely to center around rain—layers of limp, wet leaves and stomping in puddles. I've never been able to count on cold weather to ring in the holiday season. Southerners depend on more subtle signs. Counting down the number of shopping days, a mailbox stuffed with catalogues, the days getting shorter, Christmas parades, and neighbors' outdoor lights.

When I was a little girl, weather was never a factor at all in my anticipation of the holidays. I dreamed mainly of the day school let out for a two-week vacation. That was the beginning of Christmas for me. And it was usually the day the whole family squeezed in the family car and went Christmas tree hunting.

Our two-story house had high ceilings tall enough for a huge cedar tree. We'd look for the biggest tree we could find and after we got it home, daddy would nail it to a homemade wooden stand. We breathed in the spicy tang of cedar as mother brought out cardboard boxes stuffed with strings of colored lights. Not the tiny kind we use nowadays, but two-inch torches of red, blue, and green. If one light was burned out, the whole strand was dead, so we'd replace the bulbs one at a time until the chain came to life. Next we'd carefully arrange the bright balls and prickly strands of tinsel and fitfully toss silver icicles on the outstretched arms of the branches. Last came the 10-inch light-up Santa Claus who sat smiling on the tip-top of the tree. Then we "oohed and aahed" at the winking hues and agreed it was the most beautiful tree ever.

The next day we started on the giant tree in the front yard. It was the same routine with a taller ladder and outdoor lights. In those days, not many people had outside decorations and townsfolk would ride by and marvel at the sight.

Then the hectic rush of holiday preparation was at its peak. The arrival of the fat magical mail order Sears, Roebuck catalogue was almost as good as Santa Claus sliding down the chimney.

Every nook and cranny of our house held the aroma of sugar, spices, and butter as Mama started her Christmas cooking. First, she baked molasses crinkles, Toll House cookies, and gingerbread men with powdered sugar faces. Later, she'd make the cakes and ambrosia, and start the preparation for Christmas dinner.

Cards with paintings of the Nativity waited on the dining room table to be signed, sealed, and delivered.

Almost before I knew it, it was Christmas Eve, and it never seemed to matter that the next morning when I peered out the upstairs bay window, the world would be lush and green.

Christmas Nightmare

I watched the 1940-something colorized version of "A Christmas Carol" last night while I munched on wedges of cold pepperoni pizza. I dozed off about the time Tiny Tim called out, "God bless us everyone," and this is what I dreamed.

CHRISTMAS PAST: It was Christmas Eve, and I was shopping in downtown Auburn. It must have been sometime in the '50s because the mannequins in the windows at Parker's and Poly-Tek wore Poodle skirts, cashmere sweaters, Villager blouses with Peter Pan collars, and silk scarves.

I pounded the pavement searching store windows for presents I could buy with my few dollar bills. There were penny loafers on display at the Bootery, and Olin Hill's shop exhibited skinny ties and suits with thin lapels. I checked out the perfume and boxes of candy at Toomer's Drug Store before I strolled around the corner to Crest's Five and Dime Store to look at the toys.

Maybe I needed to relax awhile I thought, so I jaywalked over to Herbert Music Store to listen to my favorite LPs. But when I left, there was a package under my arm. I'd spent my money on myself. I just couldn't resist the new Johnny Mathis Christmas album.

Some change jingled in my pocket, so I carelessly crossed the street and headed for Barney's Cub Café. I slid into a padded leather booth, ordered a Coke and dropped my last dime in the jukebox. The singer warbling about the wretchedness of life matched my mood to a tee.

I was tossing and turning and in a cold sweat. I woke up enough to be jarred out of my childhood, but I fell back asleep dreaming about CHRISTMAS PRESENT.

It's about 6:30 at night and my family has finished eating supper. "Let's go visit the grandbabies," my husband suggests. As soon as we get there, I realize something is wrong. Christmas music drifts from the boom-box and the children are making gingerbread men. There's a Christmas tree decorated with twinkling lights. Underneath the tree are presents wrapped in shiny paper and big red and green bows. Seven stockings are hanging from the mantle.

"Have you finished wrapping your presents?" my daughter asks. And it hits me what's wrong. I forgot about Christmas. We don't have a tree or presents. It's Christmas Eve and the stores closed at six.

I screamed and woke up. But I drifted back into never-never-land, and this time I dreamed about CHRISTMAS FUTURE.

It's the night before Christmas, and I'm sitting at my state-of-the-art computer terminal. I type in "Christmas tree" and a giant white fir decorated in tiny sparkling white lights, white angels and white Christmas balls rises up out of the floor.

I type "Santa," and the fat man in a red suit appears on the display screen. "What do my significant others want for Christmas?" I ask. He gives me a complete list of gifts and the e-mail addresses of the appropriate stores. I enter the data, and instantly my personal shopper shows up at the door and puts my professionally wrapped presents under the tree.

I moaned and got off the couch, afraid to go back to sleep.

And I vowed never to go to sleep again after I've watched "A Christmas Carol" and munched on cold pizza.

Motherhood

God must love mothers. He's made so many of us. I don't have any statistics to quote, but I'm pretty sure that ours is not only the oldest profession on earth but the most abundant.

Somehow I find that a comforting idea. There's something soothing about the thought that I'm one of a huge, ancient sorority, each of us drawn toward much the same goals. All of us doing our level best, no matter how tough it may be, to keep the world spinning steadily on its axis by such simple missions as getting meals to the table on time, kissing skinned elbows and walking the floors at night.

Because we grow up untrained for our assignments, shoved without education into the most difficult of jobs, we sometimes belittle our calling. We don't draw a salary, go on strike, demand shorter or more regular hours, or join professional organizations. And none of us has received an honorary doctorate for mothering.

But ours is a profession we should be proud of. While physicians were still witch doctors and writers were merely minstrels, mothers existed much like we do today. We took charge of the children as well as the home, whether it was a teepee, wattle-and-daub hut, castle or a log cabin in the clearing.

And nowadays we have millions of contemporary kin. That Yanomamo woman in Venezuela stirring her pot over an open fire shares our duties and dreams. So do our cousins in Latvia or the Hebrides Islands, Wyoming or Timbuktu. In Segovian casas, Alaskan igloos, ghetto tenements and split-foyer mansions—wherever children come home to eat or sleep or talk or be comforted.

I've been a mother for more than a quarter of a century, and I've learned a lot through trial and error. Young mothers, listen up:

The quickest way to cure a child's sore throat is to tell him he's missed the school bus.

If your 10-year-old jumps up from the table to get started on homework, it's probably her turn to do the dishes.

Don't ever become too complacent. If you've never found a melted Snicker Bar in the glove box of the car or Juicy Fruit gum matted in your child's lovely locks, just wait. You will.

Any woman who finishes the laundry isn't a mother.

If you haven't combed your hair, put on lipstick or changed out of your pajamas, it's your morning to drive the carpool.

A stitch in time means remembering at the last minute where you put the needle and thread.

Never think of children as small adults. Do grown-ups drink whole bottles of cough syrup just to see what will happen? Do they sleep with a rock? Do they slosh through puddles on purpose? Or prefer butter-and-sugar sandwiches to shrimp scampi? Or beg to have *Little Bear's Visit* read to them five times a day for months? And, of course, children are quicker, smarter and in a better state of preservation than their elders.

Above all, hangest thou in there, sister. It really is worth it.

Nobody so far has won a Nobel Prize for making her home a place of such peace that her children might rise up and call her blessed—if such a strange idea ever crossed their minds.

Unfortunately, most of us don't appreciate our mothers as we should. We take them much too much for granted, like Mark Twain, who commented, "My mother had a great deal of trouble with me, but I think she enjoyed it."

Native Thanksgiving

Eyes closed, picturing what our history books tell us about the first Thanksgiving, my slide show stops on the Native Americans who were supposedly sitting around the feasting table.

That was half a millennium ago, when my Creek Indian ancestors on my daddy's side lived in the piney woods of what's now Barbour County in South Alabama. They were going about their lives spear hunting, falling in love, birthing babies, speaking their Muskhogean language, and mourning their dead. They had no notion of an Atlantic Ocean, nor any idea that there were people living on the other side of it.

At the same time, Irish peasants—my daddy's other people—scratching a living out of the rocky fields and speaking Gaelic were hardly aware of Queen Elizabeth I, much less the likelihood of America.

But somewhere in my family tree, their worlds randomly met head on in the early 19th Century. I'm sure most folks in those days mistrusted the strangers in their neck of the thicket. Each ethnocentric group thought its own ways were the best. They must have hungered for the security of past days and wished each other gone.

Lucky for me, there were some who dared to look beyond the borders of their own lineage and join together to forge a new way. And part of their new-fashioned life most likely included an American Thanksgiving Day ritual, the gathering of family at the banquet table.

By the time I came along a century and a half later, my parents had purchased a walnut dining table from an estate sale in New Orleans. And every Thanksgiving centered around that table and the food Mama made.

For days before Thanksgiving, the family kitchen was a frenzy of clanging and banging pots and pans. Things that could be made ahead were measured and sifted, simmered and stirred. Whiffs of nutmeg and cinnamon and fresh oranges tickled my nose. For this meal Mama used real butter in place of margarine, and stewed a hen to get broth and giblets for gravy.

When the day finally came, she spread the platters and bowls out buffet-style on the kitchen counter where we served our plates. On special occasions such as this, we'd cover the table with an eggshell white linen tablecloth and napkins that had the soft scent of Tide and sunshine. There were fine china dishes and, instead of the usual jelly glasses, crystal goblets.

When I was a teenager, my sisters would come with their husbands and babies, and we'd squeeze highchairs in between the stuffed straight-backed seats. By the end of the meal someone would moan, "This tablecloth will never be white again." But Mama always managed to get it clean before Christmas.

Sometimes I wonder if the descendants of my Creek ancestors who walked West on the Trail of Tears celebrate Thanksgiving too.

Old Fashioned Fourth of July

In my dream, I'm five years old again and it's a mid-summer day at our rock cabin on the river. Mama and Daddy and all us children are getting ready for a big Corbitt family Fourth of July celebration. Mama's six sisters and their families are there too.

While the Aunts tend to the last minute food preparation, Mama supervises the making of home-churned ice cream in an old ice-bucket freezer. She's already stood over the hot stove stirring the sweet egg custard until it's thick. Impatient, I come inside and watch her pour the cooled creamy mixture into the metal cylinder. Then she carefully inserts the wooden churn.

Finally, the cousins bang out side doors and gather on the stone steps where the canister is fit into the bucket and the churn-handle is locked in place.

Mama alternates ice and rock salt, filling the shaft. She places a folded dishtowel over the top to keep the ice from melting too fast, and we take turns cranking the handle. "Keep a steady rhythm," Mama instructs us. "And don't turn it backward."

The churn creaks and scrapes while water from the melting ice trickles out of a small hole partway up the bucket. Every few minutes Mama turns the handle to see if it's ready. When the crank won't budge another half-twist, Mama removes the cover being careful to keep the salt out of the ice cream. We all shout, "I choose the dasher." But, of course, we know the procedure. Mama places the dasher on a porcelain platter and hands each child a spoon. Elbows bumping, I greedily try to scoop up more than my share.

Noontime dinner is noisy. I'm as happy as a hungry hyena in a field of lambs. Two long tables are crammed with bowls of fresh vegetables, and there are homegrown tomatoes, peeled and sliced.

As we dig in, scarfing down crispy fried chicken, potato salad, deviled eggs and pitchers of sweet tea, we talk nonstop, mouths full. We sit wherever there's an empty spot, finishing up with peach cobbler topped with the hand-cranked vanilla ice cream.

Stuffed, I go down the hill and push back and forth on the rope-and-board swing. I glance up at my aunts and uncles sitting on the porch in clusters of twos and threes, fanning themselves with cardboard hardware-store fans. Their soft voices are interrupted by sporadic bursts of laughter.

After a while Mama says we can swim, so we splash in the 6-and-1/2 by 8-foot cement pool. Cold water on a July day. Aaahh. We stay until our fingers shrivel up like grapes left too long in the sun.

Late-afternoon everybody loads up to head home before dark. I can't escape the hard hugs. "Bye, Little Mary." My "Aint" Mary crushes me with an embrace.

"Ouch," I say waking up. Fifty years have passed and that pain is a stiff joint.

I can't remember the last time I celebrated the Fourth of July that way. I think this year I'll try slowing down the pace. Get together with my family. Dig out the old hand-turned ice cream freezer, and forget about fat grams.

Thankfulness

How many days do we wake up and say, "I'm so thankful my teeth don't hurt"? Or when was the last time you thought, "I'm so grateful all my children have survived chicken pox"? It rarely even crosses my mind to be happy my dog is housebroken. It's not until I get a toothache, or my child gets sick, or the schnauzer throws up on the rug that I realize how pleased I should have been.

I just assume there'll be water coming out of the faucet, heat coming out of the vent, and tasty morsels to scarf down three times a day. I don't spend a lot of time being thrilled when I turn the ignition key and the car cranks right up. It's only when I re-read James Herriot's *All Creatures Great and Small* that I'm glad about my car. "I had a puncture most days and had become an expert at changing wheels. The surface of the crumpled tyre was quite smooth except for the frayed parts where the canvas showed through," Herriot says. Later he explains, "Freezing feet were the rule in those days before car heaters, especially when you could see the road flashing past through the holes in the floorboards." Then triumphantly, "I just bought a wonderful new invention—a couple of strands of wire mounted on a strip of bakelite and fastened to the windscreen with rubber suckers. It worked on the car batteries and cleared a small space of vision."

For most of life, nothing remarkable happens. If you're not satisfied with your job and sitting down to a good meal with family and friends, then chances are you're not going to be very contented. If you base your thankfulness quotient on winning the lottery or wintering in the south of France, you aren't going to be thankful much of the time. If, on the other hand, thankfulness depends on a good breakfast, an afternoon nap, and flowers in the yard, then we are more likely to live with quite a bit of thankfulness.

My daddy once told me he'd noticed that those who were miserable in their jobs were equally unhappy in retirement. People who liked their work, he went on to say, also enjoyed retirement. And it dawns on me that daily gratitude is a must for a satisfied life.

Most of us go through the days and weeks forgetting how blessed we are. Fact is if you have food in the refrigerator, clothes in the closet, money in the bank, and change in your pocket you're one of the richest people in the world.

I recall a few years back when I was in a meeting the week before Thanksgiving. Someone suggested we go around the circle and say something we were thankful for. Most of us called out the usual "family, health, and home."

But one young woman, after a pensive pause, said, "I'm happy that I have running water." That's the only time I've heard anyone express gratitude for something so seemingly commonplace and unremarkable.

As I ponder my degree of gratefulness for small things, I'm aware that this skill doesn't come naturally for me. But with practice and perseverance maybe it will grow. On the spiral path to thankfulness, I'll do my best to make gratitude active rather than passive.

The trick is to stop and be thankful occasionally, during ordinary times— think about how good things are going. So when Thanksgiving Day gets here and my teeth don't hurt, and the children are okay, and the dog is sprawled out on the hearth snoring, I'm going to sit around and be delighted.

Thanksgiving Pageant

Lying on the couch sleeping off too much turkey always causes me to roam the old stomping grounds of holidays past.

I haven't seen a full-blown Thanksgiving pageant in years. Could be the ones I remember never really happened. But I have this vision of dressing up and acting out the first Thanksgiving.

It must have been in Mrs. Metzger's third grade. Seems most things I recall from my grammar school days were in third grade, which is a pretty good indication that most of my memories are a few pages short of a novel.

Back then, we didn't know that our history books lied to us, so we acted out the story of our forefathers and foremothers based on the gospel according Houghton-Mifflin.

Sharon Sims played Pocahontas, the beautiful Indian princess, and she got to marry tall handsome John Smith who was played by Bobby Beaird. Ken Autrey, wrapped in a blanket, was the wise and noble Chief Powatan.

It was easy to tell the Pilgrims from the Indians. One group wore paper Pilgrim hats; the other had on homemade headbands with Blue Jay feathers stapled on fitfully.

Sylvia Hollis, Carolyn Waller, Johnny Manning, Martha Ellis, Billy Lowe and other fair-haired third graders played the Pilgrims. Susan Kay, Margaret Goodman, Tom Sparrow, Morris Stoker and I were the Indians.

The script must have gone something like this:

THE VERY FIRST THANKSGIVING

SCENE ONE (The only one) Some Pilgrims are slumped around low tables. Capt. John Smith stands as Chief Powatan, Pocahontas, and a slew of Indians enter from the cloakroom.

FIRST PILGRIM: Look! Some Native Americans!

POWATAN: How.

SMITH: Funny, that's just what I was gonna ask you. How in the Queen's name are we supposed to celebrate Thanksgiving? We haven't had a crust of crumpet in three days. This is a barren area with poor soil and harsh winters, offering little chance for our survival.

POWATAN: This is y'all's lucky day. We're fresh out of crumpets, but we have a plethora of turkey, cornbread dressing with giblet gravy, cranberry sauce, peas-and-asparagus casserole and pumpkin pie.

SECOND PILGRIM: Yuk! Let's call out for pizza.

THIRD PILGRIM: Don't be a geek. You know phones haven't been invented yet. Anyway, I'm having a Big Mac attack.

FIRST NATIVE AMERICAN: (Rolling his eyes at the two bickering Pilgrims) Fortunately, we speak perfect English and are here to help you.

SMITH: Good. Bring on the feast. (Turning to Powatan) By the way, I'm going to marry your traffic-stopping-gorgeous daughter.

SECOND NATIVE AMERICAN: Over my dead body.

SMITH: That's kinda what I had in mind.

(The Pilgrims jump up from the table and begin pushing, shoving, biting, and in general, scratching the eyes out of the Native Americans.)

FOURTH PILGRIM: (With his fingers wrapped around Powatan's throat, turns to Capt. Smith) Hey, I thought we were gonna eat!

And you know the rest of the story. The original inhabitants of this land have been immortalized as filthy savages.

Pondering

"I had a stick of CareFree gum,
but it didn't work. As soon
as the gum lost its flavor,
I went back to pondering."

Source Unknown

Exits

As I sat sipping the last hot swallow of my coffee this morning, I turned on the Today Show. While I half-heartedly watched, I remembered that Katie Couric had left the show for the CBS Evening News, and her departure set me pondering partings.

Songwriter Paul Simon said there are fifty ways to leave your lover. There are also at least 50 ways to leave your job, your parents, your children, a dull party, Jordan-Hare Stadium or a state of mind. Exits and partings are the subjects of novels, plays, songs, and poems.

In the old Western movies Roy Rogers rode into the sunset singing "Happy Trails To You" and The Lone Ranger galloped off in a cloud of dust leaving folks wondering "Who was that masked man?"

Our own parting lines reveal different senses of closure. "So long" is informal and carefree. "Farewell" indicates a wish for the other person to go on under favorable conditions. "Adieu" is a French term that literally means "to God" as if the person saying good-bye is leaving the other in God's care.

When we leave a person, place or state of mind we stand at the brink of giving up something familiar for something that isn't yet real. And most of us dread the unknown.

I've had plenty of exits in my time. Hundreds have faded into a fog of the past. Some have stayed as clear and fresh as a mountain stream. I recall my first significant departure—leaving my birthplace in West Point, Georgia to move to Auburn when I was seven years old. I sat submerged to the neck in bath water when I got the news we were leaving the only home I'd ever known. And I sobbed broken-hearted tears as if trying to turn the tub-water brackish.

Later, when we left, I watched sad-eyed as the red rocking horse I'd long-since outgrown was left on the curb because there was no more room in the moving van. With that move I began to learn the hard lesson that leaving means passage, not always into a dark cave, but mostly into a tunnel with a light at the end. After all, the stifling days of summer pass on to become cool September nights. And hasn't it been said that the night is darkest before the dawn?

As I sit here in my squeaky office chair, I ruminate on a different version of my life. And suddenly, my mind, though I hadn't asked it to, has made me a spectator of my own biography; has relentlessly shown me pictures of who I might have been.

What if I had never left the tiny town in Georgia? What if I'd gone to the University of Colorado instead of Auburn? What if the Vietnam War hadn't influenced the choices I made in my early twenties?

Not long ago as I flipped through an anthropology textbook I spotted the name Sharlotte K. Neely. "Hey," I said out loud. "She's that ditzy person from grad school. I was a lot smarter than that girl. How come she's quoted in this book instead of me?"

It's easy to let the what-ifs and who-I-might-have-been parade down the sidewalk of my past turning corners where I went straight. I've gone through lots of doors, and I've had some slammed in my face. I'll probably never know if the paths I chose were the best ones to take.

But one thing I've learned is not to be too sad over partings. Every exit is an entry to somewhere else.

Fast Time—Slow Time

We live in a decade that seems to worship speed—fast food, Interstate driving, and outpatient gall bladder surgery. We're far too busy to linger over a long, languid supper. Instead, we bolt a quick meal and rush out the door to the next event.

Let me point out that I'm as bad as the next 21st Century harried woman. I dash off a hurried email, or better yet, a skimpy text. And I rarely have a long phone conversation.

I remember slower times as if they happened last week. A fine summer morning sitting on the screened-in-porch scratching my Cocker Spaniel between the ears. It was a whole different world, writing and receiving long, gossipy letters. Sending a missive to a friend or kinfolk on vacation was just a matter of course. If I got a long distance call, I knew there was an emergency.

As a child I helped Mama hang clothes on the line outside the back door. I carried the canvas bag of wooden pins and handed them to her one at a time. Some days we'd take a leisurely walk to the library. And in the afternoon when she put together time consuming recipes, I sat on the kitchen counter watching and waiting for a spoon to lick.

Years later, when I was a grownup with a kitchen of my own, I baked crusty loaves of wheat bread, measuring a bit of yeast into a bowl of warm water and dumping in flour. I learned to knead, putting the dough on a floured surface, pushing, folding it over and pushing it again, each time turning it a quarter turn. I'd drink tea while it rose, then punch it down again until it was ready to bake.

I made chicken soup that started with a butter and flour roux, stirring constantly until it was just the right thickness. I added the boiled chicken I'd pulled from the bone and the onion I'd minced, and finally mixed in a pint of cream, not milk. On an ordinary Thursday night I'd make Carbanade, a specialty of Northern France. Tuesday I might spend time chopping vegetables for Brennan's Gumbo or Sweet-and-Sour Pork. These days, I don't take the time to make quick breads and my chicken soup comes from a can.

Technology has made all manner of things too easy. Why go to the library when you can flip open your Kindle and have the book ready to read in a minute? Why sit and watch a television movie when you can record it and fast-forward the commercials?

When I was growing up, people who lived in East Alabama and worked in West Georgia, or the other way around, called the different time zones "fast time" and "slow time." Nowadays those terms have taken on a whole new meaning for me. I used to live in slow time. Now I live in fast time. It's as simple as that.

Fears

What would I do if I had nothing to fear? As a child, it seems I had no fears. Like a Marine recruit following a drill Sgt., I fell in behind my big sister Jane without question. It never occurred to me that danger might lurk ahead. She led me down steep hills on rickety roller skates. The skate key hung from a string around my neck flying in the wind, as much a symbol of bravado as the Red Baron's scarf.

We raced along the banks of the Chattahoochee River, through boggy underbrush, not the least bit daunted by water moccasins that watched us from beneath rotting leaves. We climbed to the top of the monster slide at Felton Little Park, sat on sheets of waxed paper, and rushed recklessly to the ground faster than greased lightening.

I don't know when fears began creeping into my life. Could've been the moment my Mama dropped her handbag from a ledge at the top of Mount Mitchell, the highest point in North Carolina, and I watched helplessly the everlasting loss of an inanimate object. I remember the queasy dizziness I felt as the purse spiraled into the abyss, becoming smaller and smaller until, almost invisible, it collided with a rock. And evermore, I experience that same blurred vision, my stomach rising into my throat, when I stand at the crest of a mountain face.

Or maybe my sense of unease came to a head in my teen years, that time in my life when the most frightening thing of all was the fear of not fitting in, of being different. Being myself. That sort of soul-numbing dread is stifling, worse than the tangible kind like the fear of flying, public speaking, venomous snakes, or axe murderers.

Over the years I've done a ton of things that scare me. I've jumped a horse over high fences, maneuvered a metal Jon boat through reptile infested swamp-waters, and walked half the length of a football field between two ropes that were stretched taut across a 200-foot ravine. I've sailed the Chesapeake Bay in stormy weather and learned the basics of mountain climbing on a sheer cliff.

I must've been adhering to John Wayne's credo that "Courage is being scared to death and saddling up anyway."

Still, more often than not, I'm cowardly and fainthearted. My anxieties pile up, overruling the memory of times that I've stepped out in faith and lived to tell about it. And I see that I've become too careful. Too calculated and guarded.

But I think of Jawaharlal Nehru's warning that the policy of being too cautious is the greatest risk of all. He was right, of course. I'm sure the things

I try to avoid are precisely the things I need to do to keep me growing. So I've decided to work on overcoming my fears one baby step at a time.

Maybe I'll bombard myself with challenging people and situations. Shake myself up with dangerous ideas. Push the limits, and get out of my comfort zone. I just might go back to wearing a skate key around my neck as a reminder.

How to be a Grandmother

Now that I'm a grandmother, it seems to me that grandmothers are a lot younger than they used to be.

I only knew one of my grandmothers, and she died when I was very young. My other grandparents died before I was born, so I never had much practice being a grandchild. And I didn't have a grandparent for a role model.

Grandmother-hood didn't come at all naturally to me. I had no interest in being a kindly, doddering codger who smiled at everything my grandchildren did while toting around stacks of Kodak prints. My youngest child was barely nine at the time. Seemed like I was the one who should be having a baby.

But one thing comes naturally to me as a grandmother—constant worry. Writer Peter Mayle says, "A connoisseur of woe needs fresh worries from time to time, or he will become complacent." When it comes to my grandbabies, there's no chance of complacency. I watch my little grandbuddies jumping joyously on the trampoline, and I'm deaf to their shrieks of delight and blind to their radiant smiles. All I can envision as they bounce and giggle is bones crunching, teeth chipping, and brains concussing.

Freak accidents loom large in my mind. And obscure diseases that can be contracted only by the bite of a pregnant African tsetse fly to the left earlobe seem to be an ever-present danger. I scan articles about choking and wish they could be fed intravenously. And activities my own children enjoyed are on my list of things that should be strictly forbidden to my grandchildren.

I've learned a lot in the past five years. One thing I've discovered is that it's easier to learn how to be a grandchild than it is to learn how to be a grandmother. Grandchildren know instantly what to do and how to behave. And mine are patiently teaching me the things I need to know.

Five-year-old DJ is forever having to remind me to buckle my seat belt and put the jelly in the refrigerator. And I can tell by the tilt of his little blond head and his bemused voice that he can't believe I've forgotten again. When I baby-sit, I'm constantly asking him, "What time does Katherine go down for her nap?" or "Can Katherine eat peanut butter?" or "Where do Mommy and Daddy keep the trash bags?"

It's a funny thing. I don't feel like I've acquired three grandchildren so much as I feel like I've gained three tousle-haired ragamuffin friends.

I remember from watching the old Art Linkletter show that kids say the darndest things. But I'm never quite prepared for some of the things my grandchildren come up with.

Not long ago I took a walk with a 3-year-old girl-grandchild. I held her hand as we walked, and I had to stoop a little because she's so small. The child, whose name is Kristen, darted away, hair flying in the breeze, blue eyes sparkling. Her laughter sprinkled the hot air.

Then she wheeled and waited for me to catch up with her. And in that mater-of-fact tone she has, she told me, "I'm really an adult."

I gave her a blank, raised-eyebrows look, and she explained. "An adult is just a child who can stand up in the swimming pool."

I think I may be just the right age to be a grandmother after all.

Imagination

A certain girl grandbaby interrupted my newspaper scanning one afternoon. I peeped over the newsprint and watched her hook a dangling set of rusty handcuffs to my wrists. "You've got to go to jail," she said. I moaned, not having the energy to move, but when she told me that my bed was the prison, I gladly followed the three-foot jailer.

And as I lay luxuriously sprawled out in my prison cell, I pondered some of my childhood antics. My sister Jane and I shared a big double bed, and on rainy days it became a time machine for our play-like games. Like the children in C.S. Lewis' *The Lion, the Witch and the Wardrobe*, we'd climb into the bed and instantly be inhabitants of another time and place.

When the weather was too messy or cold for us to go outside and play outlaws and in-laws, we'd bring the Wild West into the bedroom. We switched easily from the Lone Ranger and Tonto or Frank and Jesse James to pioneer women crossing the plains with several babies in our covered wagon. We used our cap guns to fight off Indian raiding parties and outlaw bandits, and we circled up the wagons and cooked beans over the campfire.

Sometimes the bed became a steam locomotive transporting soldiers, a stagecoach carrying the payroll to Fort Collins, a mule-drawn Civil War ambulance, or a runaway Roman chariot. Other days it might be a paddle boat chugging down the Mississippi River, a birch bark canoe silently exploring the Pacific Northwest or a Viking warship crossing the North Atlantic Ocean.

We had to use our imaginations back then because we didn't have many toys. We had a scuffed up baseball and a heavy wooden bat, and we made a football by stuffing leaves into a mesh potato sack. There were dime store diversions like marbles, yo-yos, pickup sticks, Go Fish and Old Maid cards.

And there were games that used things you could find around the house. For "Pass the Button" you only needed one discarded button. Mumbly-peg required a small pocketknife. If we wanted to swing and slide, we walked to Felton Little Park.

My Aunt Mary owned a real game—an old croquet set. The wooden balls having been chewed by dogs and eroded by rain were no rounder than dried up oranges. The paint had chipped and faded, and the wickets were bent out of shape. We laid the course out on her back lawn happily and haphazardly, and we would go out after supper, choose mallets and play noisily with Sambo, our cocker spaniel, racing after the balls.

We never knew the rules of croquet. Never knew that the course was supposed to be exactly 72 feet long, the wickets perfectly aligned. As with our other games, we made up the rules.

When I do a mental inventory of the playthings my grandbuddies own, it's mind boggling. A Fisher-Price house and castle. Bikes and scooters. A trampoline and swing set. Gobs of indoor toys. Not to mention a television, VCR and CD player.

But never let it be said that all these material goods have dulled the ingenuity of today's children. If anything, it's made them more creative.

"Hurry," my bright-eyed jailer whispered. "I've come to help you escape."

"Do I have to? Couldn't I stay a few more minutes?"

My Bucket List

One freezing February day many years ago, my daddy came face to face with an old woman outside his office building. The raw wind tugged at his coat as drifting snowflakes melted on the bald top of his head. The woman looked him up and down and in a disgusted tone said, "Old as you is, and you ain't wearin' a hat."

I have a mental list of things that, old as I is, I ain't done. And even though I'm not planning on passing anytime soon, I think of them as things I'd like to do before I die.

This certainly isn't a new idea. In fact, it became a popular topic after the movie "Bucket List" came out in 2007. Now it seems like a lot of folks are talking about things they want to do before they die. I've even had a 17-year-old tell me about her bucket list.

My longtime list includes things like riding a horse in Central Park, writing a novel with substance, playing my French Horn in the orchestra of a Broadway Musical, hiking the Appalachian Trail, and living on an island. But it seems the older I get, the more things I want to do. And now, I find myself wanting to do all sorts of things I've never thought about before.

I read about J. Peterman and his regrets for not staying in Shepheard's Hotel in Cairo. It burned to the ground in 1952 before he could afford to check in. "That night," he said, "it became my code word for everything unobtained, undone." He mourned missing out on one perfect night at Shepheard's Hotel.

And while I think it's good to have things to look forward to, I hope I never mourn things left undone.

My mother told a story that happened to a local postman when she was growing up in Eufaula in the early part of the Twentieth Century. At that time, mailmen rode bicycles to deliver mail in rural areas. One day when the postman was making deliveries, his bicycle hit a patch of sand. The bike turned over and threw him off, knocking the wind out of him. While he was lying on the ground trying to catch his breath, a woman walked by and saw him and thought that he was dead. She noticed the grimace on his face caused by the grit in his mouth, and said, "Thank God he died with a smile on his face."

I may never ride a horse in Central Park. I'll probably never live on an island. Writing a great novel is clearly out. But if I get run over at the intersection of College Street and Glenn Avenue anytime soon, I hope folks will be able to say, "Thank God she died with a smile on her face."

Through a Child's Eyes

Okay, put on your thinking cap. Here's a mind bender to get you waked up. Sam left his tenth floor apartment every morning at 7:30. He got on the elevator, pushed the button for the first floor, and rode to the lobby. After a day's work, Sam came back to his apartment building, got on the elevator, pushed the sixth floor button, got off on the sixth floor, and walked up to his apartment on the tenth floor. Why did Sam get off on the sixth floor?

Sam wanted a little exercise? Nope. Try again. Something was wrong with the elevator and it wouldn't go past the sixth floor? Not even close.

If you've taken a three-year-old to the Haley Center lately, the answer would be obvious. Sam was a midget.

I hadn't thought about that puzzle in 20 years. Then I took a certain small grandbuddy with me to work the other day, and when we stepped into the elevator, the puzzle about Sam came flashing back. "Push seven," I told Katherine. She stood on her tiptoes, but I had to lift her up to reach the button. Coming down after my class was a whole different story. "Push one," I said. And she did.

Taking a three-year-old to work can change your world-view. Children just don't see things the way adults do. At times we miss the obvious. My friend Emily Myers' three-year-old Maddie has called the Haley Center "Mommy's Tower" for as long as she's been verbal. I thought that was unusual until I drove up to that same building with Katherine who took one look and said, "Your school is a tower."

And my sister Jane took 4-year-old Ben to Foy Union Building. They walked out on the patio to see the turtles, and after a quick glance Ben said, "That turtle's eye is hurt."

"No," she tried to explain, looking at the reptile's great glassy, bulging eyes. "Turtle's eyes just look like that."

Ben didn't budge. "His eye is hurt," he said.

Somewhere along the way adults lose that fresh way of looking at things. We learn to categorize everything. Put things in convenient little boxes, so that we hardly have to look at all. It makes our lives easier.

Then again, it complicates things in an insidious way. Causes us to think in terms of stereotypes. Makes us have prejudices. Creates intolerance if something or somebody doesn't fit in the box.

But pint-size people aren't that way. When my youngest daughter was very small, she crossed a hospital waiting room alone to sit by a man who looked like he might be hiding a sawed-off shotgun in his pants leg; an unwashed man with his head tied in a red rag. Later when I asked her why she wanted to sit by him, she said, "He looked so nice."

A child isn't bound by *Good Housekeeping's* standards about what's suitable for certain meals. If there's pizza in the fridge, it tastes as good to him for breakfast as any other time. And a youngster doesn't take a bath to get clean. If the layers of dirt happen to slide off while she's in the tub playing with rubber boats, so be it.

Maybe it's the hours kids spend hanging upside-down by their knees on the bars of jungle gyms, peering down from the lap of a dogwood branch, dangling head first off the couch, or teetering on the back legs of a chair. Could be it rearranges their vision.

If it's been a while since you took a seat on top of a gatepost to watch the world go by, try borrowing a child for the morning. All ages have their charm. And I can promise a child will reinvent your world for you.

Two Sides to Every Story

It takes two to tango. Two to argue. Two feet to walk. And my mother always said there are two sides to every story.

I tend to be a person who can see more than one point of view. For instance, not long ago a neighborhood cat was hanging out near a mockingbird nest. As soon as the mama bird laid some eggs, she started dive-bombing the tabby on a regular basis.

I took the side of the bird. After all, she was protecting her babies. I was surprised when the neighbors defended the cat—claimed the bird was harassing him. I decided to watch. When the bird followed the cat into his own carport and riveted him with machine-gun pecks, I figured the cat-owners had a point.

Sometimes words affect the way folks see things. Americans say: Our women put rings through their ears and cosmetics on their faces to enhance their beauty. Their women put bones through their noses and scars on their faces, and it makes them ugly.

We say: We don't eat cats or worms because it's cruel or disgusting. They won't eat beef because they have silly food taboos. We cover our bodies because we're decorous and civilized. They walk around naked because they're ignorant and shameless. And Middle-Eastern women cover their entire bodies because they're backward.

Our brave soldiers achieve glorious victories over enemies. Their fanatical soldiers perpetrate bloody massacres on us.

When I read *The Last Algonquin*, a beautiful true story about a boy's friendship with an old Algonquin Indian, I was convinced that the Algonquins were the noblest humans on earth. Later I happened upon *A Narrative of the Captivity of Mrs. Mary Rowlandson*. Rowlandson's 1667 journal describes the death of her minister husband at the hands of Algonquin Indians. "The murderous wretches knocked him in the head and split open his bowels." Mrs. Rowlandson was taken captive by these "hell-hounds." They set her on a bareback horse with her wounded child. "As we were going down a steep hill we both fell over the horse's head, at which they, like inhumane creatures, laughed and rejoiced to see it."

I felt sick as I scanned the narrative. Could these be the same Algonquins I'd read about? I rummaged around in Clark Wissler's *Indians of the United States*. Seems the Algonquins, including Pocahontas and Squanto, were the first to welcome the Europeans and the first to shed blood in resisting their merciless advances.

Whites burned villages, killing women and children, selling captives into slavery. The Indians retaliated. The settlers cut off the heads of those they killed and set them up on poles to enrage the Indians, who in turn tortured and scalped whites.

Truth is, both accounts I'd read about the Algonquins were true. I thought about an incident that happened a few years ago.

My grandson called me on the phone sobbing. "Kristen pinched me!" three-year-old DJ wailed, accusing his baby sister.

"Let me talk to her," I said, wondering if I could communicate over the telephone with the 15-month-old alleged culprit.

Kristen spoke loudly and indignantly into the receiver. "DJ *rnpdtfl pinch thrmpd#t NOT qxyzagrb!" I could understand enough to know she was painting a totally different picture.

I couldn't help laughing, but at the same time, it made me stop and think. It's enough to make you believe there really are two sides to every story.

Welcome to the World Baby Girl

There you lie on your daughter's sofa listening to the night sounds, your eyes fixed on the slow whirring ceiling fan, your nose breathing in the sweetish smell of peanut butter and jelly sandwiches already fixed for the children's lunches.

It's the second time you've been alerted. The first time was false labor. This must be the real thing. It's 3 a.m. and they haven't come back. You practice saying the date over and over in your head, surely this is a day you'll be celebrating from now on.

Suddenly there's a sound from the back of the house. One of the children has cried out. You stagger down the hall to check and find DJ completely covered except for one foot sticking out for air. And you have to smile because that's just how you sleep. In the next room Kristen is sprawled gracefully on her back uncovered. You pull the blanket over her and she stirs. In the next bed, Katherine with her thumb stuffed in her mouth, breathes rhythmically.

You sink into the couch again and try to think of mothers in Mali who have daughters delivering babies with no white-coated doctors or nurses and no hospitals or anesthetics to make things easier for them. Then you remember that this daughter of yours believes in natural childbirth, and the thought sends you scurrying to the kitchen to gulp down some water.

Then back to your post on the couch. You get in just the right position, but you can't sleep. On such a night you wonder what it is you normally think about when you aren't dwelling on labor pains and childbirth, on nights that were made for sleeping. You wonder if it would be better to get up and read. You might even find some chores to do. But you decide it's better to lie in the dark and listen to the crickets in the woods.

You turn to memories of the past to blot out thoughts of the present. But of course the memories are of your children's illnesses and medicines when they were growing up. Suddenly every burning fever and ear infection is as clear as a Windexed-window. And you picture the words tonsillitis, bronchitis, stitches, hairline fracture, flu, sinusitis, chickenpox, stomach virus, penicillin, strep throat, and Tylenol jumping over a split-rail fence one by one like a flock of wooly sheep.

You search your mind for more comforting thoughts. And you remember when this daughter who's having a baby was a baby. She was so tiny you carried her around on a pillow, and you walked the floor in the early morning hours humming along with the latest "Simon and Garfunkle" album hoping the music would soothe her colic. You thought those were the tough times of mothering. Now you're not so sure.

Finally you fall asleep and when the 6 o'clock alarm goes off you find your daughter has been sent home again. But 24 hours later the doctors can't put it off any longer.

This time it's daylight and there are things to be done, things that will occupy your mind. Children to get off to school and a three-year-old to tend to. Still the hours drag.

And you think it would seem more real if you were at the hospital waiting, hands cold and damp, staring at the labor room door, nurses wheeling scary-looking machines in and out, straining to hear the words as the door swings shut.

Then the call comes. The baby has decided to be born. So you pile the kids in the car and head down Opelika Road. At the hospital you weave in and out of the endless maze of halls until you find the room. And there she is in a little cotton cap, swaddled in a receiving blanket with one foot sticking out for air.

You smile happily and say heartily, "Welcome to the world, baby girl!"

Little Known History

"To remain ignorant of things that
happened before you were born
is to remain a child."

Cicero

African-American Jockeys

I nosed my Hyundai into a slot beneath an ancient oak at Hopeland Park in Aiken, South Carolina. As I strolled into the Thoroughbred Racing Hall of Fame, I thought I'd be doing nothing more than enjoying an hour of equine memorabilia. Instead, I was delighted by a morning of enlightenment, not about horses, but about the roles of African-Americans in horseracing.

Once inside the museum, I learned that more than a century before Jackie Robinson broke the color barrier in major league baseball, black athletes dominated American's first national sport. The sport was horse racing, and the greatest jockeys were slaves and the sons of slaves.

I borrowed a pencil and piece of paper from the volunteer at the front desk and started feverishly taking notes on Isaac Murphy, the most famous of the black jockeys. He was the first jockey to win three Kentucky Derbys and won an amazing 44% of all the races he rode. That record has never been approached by any other jockey. "Honest Ike" was the first jockey inducted into the Jockey Hall of Fame, and many say he's the greatest jockey in American History.

I moved on to Ansel Williamson who was born a slave. He trained Aristides, the Thoroughbred who won the first Kentucky Derby in 1875. Oliver Lewis, a black jockey, rode Aristides to a two-length upset victory in that inaugural Derby.

African-American equestrian Alonzo "Lonnie" Clayton won the Kentucky Derby as a 15-year-old in 1892. The only other jockey to win the Derby at that young age was James "Soup" Perkins, another black rider. And there was Willie Simms who won the Derby twice and each of the Triple Crown races at least once. Simms was one of the first successful jockeys using the short-stirrup style that all jockeys use these days.

If I knew how to write a screenplay, I'd make a movie about Jimmy "Wink" Winkfield. History kept Winkfield from becoming America's greatest racing phenomenon. Wink endured racism, exile, the Russian Revolution, and two World Wars. He was the last black jockey to win the Kentucky Derby. After winning back to back Derbies in 1901 and 1902, Thoroughbred owners switched to white riders, and blacks were hired as stable help. So Wink boarded a steamer, emigrating to Europe where he had a profitable racing career riding for Russia's Czar Nicholas II. He became fluent in several languages and married a Russian heiress before he retired with over 2500 wins.

The accomplishments of African-American horsemen in the early years of racing have been all but forgotten. The glory-days ranged from the 1700s to the early 1900s. The memory of these great black athletes has been erased from history. It's the story of a young country where whole towns showed up in cleared fields to cheer and place bets on magnificent horses and the men who rode them. It's about a nation whose greatest athletes were slaves dressed in colorful silks. This is the most fascinating untold sports story in American History.

Black West

Huge chunks of my childhood were spent riding a pretend pinto pony across a make-believe Western landscape. Such pastimes weren't unusual for kids back then. Most of us went to Saturday matinees, sat spellbound and watched our heroes riding, shooting, and guzzling sarsaparilla.

When William Katz started a book on black history in the 1960s, he called Langston Hughes and asked if he could quote from his writings. Hughes said, "Yes," then added one piece of advice, "Don't leave out the cowboys."

Those Westerns we were so fond of showed only Anglo-American cowboys. Black frontiersmen, cowpokes, and gunslingers riding across the western plains were neglected in books. Engravings of settlers crossing the prairie showed only whites. This created the myth that blacks had no part in settling the frontier. Although black adventurers, wranglers, and homesteaders traveled the length and breadth of this land, they were omitted when history was put into print. But they are mentioned in explorers' diaries, government reports, pioneers' journals and frontier newspapers.

Five thousand black men helped drive cattle up the Chisholm Trail. A trail crew of eight usually included two black cowpunchers. By 1890, there were half a million black men, women and children living in Texas and Oklahoma. Mostly ordinary folks trying to earn a living, their lives were hard and lonely, not ones of adventure.

J. H. Brewer rode with "Colonel Fant's Dark Cowboys." Fant had a government contract to furnish beef in the Indian Territory. He hired a hundred black cowhands to drive his herds up the trail every year.

Charlie Glass, a broncobuster and cowpuncher, became a foreman of his outfit. And a photograph of the JJ Ranch crew with their chuck wagon shows several black cattlemen.

"Peerless" Jessie Stahl was considered the best rider of wild horses in the West. Bill Pickett, a rodeo performer, developed "bulldogging" into an art. He was assisted by two unknown cowpunchers, Tom Mix and Will Rogers. One ranch owner called him "the greatest sweat and dirt cowhand that ever lived—bar none."

In 1887, black cowboy Arizona Joe became a hero in a five-cent Western novel.

If you're looking for more colorful stories, there are plenty of those too. Life in the West was dangerous and often short. The first man shot in Dodge City was a black cowboy named Tex, an innocent bystander to a fight between two whites.

Nat Love, known as "Deadwood Dick," was adopted by an Indian tribe, rode bareback 100 miles in 12 hours, was shot 14 times, and was good friends with Bat Masterson.

Cherokee Bill was the black counterpart to Billy the Kid, and Ben Hodges earned his keep playing cards in Dodge City alongside Wyatt Earp.

One of the most powerful characters to ride the Rocky Mountain Pony Express trails was gun toting Mary Fields. In her 60s, she carried the mail, never hindered by weather or terrain.

Pictures and documents substantiate the truth. Unlike so many western tales, these are no campfire yarns.

First Americans

All the hype about Christopher Columbus discovering America mangles my fur. There's even a national holiday commemorating the event.

Problem is, Columbus didn't discover America. It wasn't lost. In fact, Columbus was the one who was lost. He thought he was in the distant Indies, somewhere between Japan and India, for crying out loud. That's why he called the natives Indians.

The New World was anything but empty when Columbus arrived. The first Americans crossed a glacial land bridge between Siberia and Alaska more than 12,000 years ago. By 1492, the Western Hemisphere may have contained 90 million people. Ancient societies had been rising and falling here for centuries.

When Chris Columbus and his band of merry men stepped ashore, the local people met him on the beach saying, "Ooh Nay thla Nah, he oo way gee," which translated means, "There goes the neighborhood."

And at that moment the natives began the thankless, tedious task of teaching the Europeans how to become civilized. Newcomers from Europe were accustomed to people being burned at the stake or beheaded, but they were appalled at the alien customs of the natives. One practice the Europeans particularly hated was the Native Americans' habit of taking a daily bath.

Three centuries before the U.S. Constitution was adopted, the Iroquois League had a Congress-like council, exercised the veto, protected freedom of speech, and ran a classless society. Most tribes had councils to govern them. Our founding fathers modeled the United States government after the Iroquois League that emphasized equal rights for all individuals.

The hundreds of Native Americans languages, spoken by as many diverse cultures, were as different from one another as Swahili is from French. Some Native Americans were warriors; many abhorred fighting. When Arizona's Pimas were forced to fight, the warriors were subjected to a 16-day cure for insanity.

A Southwestern Zuni woman could end a marriage at any time by placing her husband's belongings outside the door to show that he was no longer welcome. But if an Alabama Creek Indian had an extra-marital affair, it would cost her a nose or an ear.

The Arawaks showered Columbus with gifts of cloth, fish, turkeys, and persimmon bread. Their generosity was interpreted as a sign that the natives were childlike. And the fact that the natives didn't accumulate wealth was seen as laziness.

The settlers couldn't have survived without the Native Americans. Besides foods, such as corn and tomatoes, and medicines made of herbs, roots, bark and leaves, the natives were the first to cultivate cotton, use rubber, toboggans, snowshoes, panchos, hammocks, and canoes. They were also advanced in pottery making and sculpture.

Twenty years after Columbus colonized Hispaniola, diseases reduced the Arawaks from a quarter-million to fewer than 20,000. In a short time Old World diseases such as smallpox and chickenpox killed millions of New World natives. Many tribes had death rates of up to 90 percent.

In less than 500 years we managed to kill off the buffalo, break every treaty, take all the good land, and still portray Native Americans as the savages. But that's all right. They gave us tobacco.

Horace Pippin

This isn't at all what I started out to write. But I'm beginning to learn that sometimes writing has a mind of its own. I was just trying to find some new stuff for Black History Month when I stumbled across a book on Horace Pippin. And as I read, it occurred to me that this artist might very well be an African-American Everyman.

Seems Pippin's pencil had a mind of its own too. As a boy growing up in the late 1800s, every time the teacher called out a spelling word, his pencil drew pictures. She said, "Dog," and Horace wrote D-O-G and drew a picture right after the letter G. "Stove," she called out. He spelled S-T-O-V-E, but before he knew it there was a picture of a stove. Every day, his teacher made him stay after school to re-do his lesson. And he knew full well that when he got home he'd get a spanking for being late.

When he was ten, Horace entered a magazine contest. "Make Me And Win A Prize," said big letters under a picture of a funny face. Horace drew the picture and sent it in. The next week the prize came in the mail: a box of paint, two brushes, and six colored pencils. So he began a lifetime of painting that lasted until his death in 1946.

During World War I, Horace joined the all-black New York 15th National Guard Regiment. With no weapons or training they were shipped to France.

Horace's unit spent six months in the front-line trenches, and his pictures of those days show men suffering unimaginable hardships. The sketches are simple, but they tell a terrible tale.

One morning as Horace dove for cover, a sniper shot him in the shoulder. He stayed there bleeding, too weak to move, until the next day when rescuers put him on a stretcher, where he lay in the rain all day and night until he could be taken to a field hospital.

When Pippin returned home there was no job for him. He could move his pencil but not his shriveled right arm, so for 11 years there were no sketches. Then one winter day, he took the poker from the potbellied stove and placed the red-hot tip to an extra leaf from the oak table. He balanced the poker on his knee and moved the wood around with his strong left arm. And like a magician, he etched images into the wood. He created incredible burnt-wood panels for a decade until the longing to paint haunted his mind.

Pippin couldn't afford artists' materials so he scavenged the neighborhood for tossed out cans of house paint, and heavy cotton fabric to use as canvases. He held the brush in his right hand, guiding it with his left. After 10 years, he sold 25 painting and was on his way to fame. Critics loved his "singing colors" and "imaginative patterns." Today his work is on display at the Smithsonian Institution and The Metropolitan Museum of Art.

But I had to dig deep to uncover Horace Pippin. And I'm mighty glad I found him—the self-taught artist who, with pencil, paintbrush, and poker told his life story better than any poet.

Negro League

"When you were a kid, what did you want to be when you grew up?" Ask any man of my generation and without missing a beat, he'll tell you, "I wanted to be a major league baseball player."

My dream as a barefoot girl was the same. But unlike my male counterparts, I can claim discrimination foiled my plans. "The reason I didn't make it to the big league was because I was a girl," I protest. Then I smugly point out, "You weren't good enough."

There's another group of ball players, men who were good enough to play in the majors but whose opportunities were denied. They were African Americans excluded from the National Association of Baseball Players, because the game had been designed for and was played by white, middle-class men. There was an unwritten "gentlemen's agreement" in the mid-1850s, the first drawing of the color line in baseball.

Refusing to let their dreams dry up, black ball players formed the Negro Baseball League in 1867. Most of us don't know much about those teams or their legends. Ever heard of John "Bud" Fowler? As a boy, poet Carl Sandburg saw Fowler play an entire game at second base left-handed. White sportswriters called him, "One of the best pitchers in America."

What about catcher Brother Welday or Bert "Yellow Kid" Jones the fireballing lefthander who pitched for Atchison? Do the names Sol White, Turkey Stearnes, Bid McPhee, Moses "Fleet" Walker, or Rube Foster ring a bell? I didn't think so.

There was George "Mule" Suttles who played for St. Louis. And outfielder Cool Papa Bell was so fast some said, "If he bunts and the ball bounces twice you just put it in your pocket."

Ted "Double Duty" Radcliffe was an all-star on several teams. With his solid build he made a natural catcher, but his strong throwing arm helped him develop into a dominant and crafty pitcher. Famous sportswriter Damon Runyon watched him play in a doubleheader. He caught the first game and pitched the second. "A player worth the price of two admissions," Runyon wrote.

Catcher Josh Gibson, hit homeruns that broke the backs of wooden seats in the upper deck. Fast as lightening, he said, "When I come to the plate, I'm in scoring position." "Black Diamond" Gibson may have been the greatest slugger of all time. He could hit .400 like Ted Williams and had the power of Babe Ruth.

And no pitcher can be compared to Satchel Paige. Satchel could throw the ball 110 miles an hour. He struck out Rogers Hornsby five times in an exhibition game, and Joe DiMaggio called him the greatest pitcher he ever faced.

Negro League all-star squads barnstormed against farm teams, prison teams, women's squads, and even major league all-stars. They played constantly, traveling hundreds of miles a day in cramped cars and swaying buses. They wore baggy uniforms made of heavy wool. A player had only one uniform that he washed on his day off.

Negro League ball was fast and loose with teams that bunted often and ran the bases like madmen. Pitchers were tough and wily.

They knew they could play in the big leagues because they played the major leaguers and beat them. Man, how I'd love to have seen that.

Saluting Women

Women's History Month is a time to salute our founding mothers. Seems there have been several waves of the women's movement in this country. But the most amazing thing is that, if you look at it from an historical perspective, women's rights have come such a long way in such a short time.

In the 1890s women were considered the legal property of men. They had no rights. Laws began to change that year, and in Texas, the Legislature raised the age of sexual consent from 7 to 10. But for years the laws changed at a turtle's pace. The Texas Constitution mandated, until 1918, that all Texans had the right to vote except "idiots, imbeciles, aliens, the insane and women." Even after women could vote, they weren't allowed to serve on juries until the mid-1950s.

Many states had an article in their penal codes that made it legal for a husband who found his wife and her lover in a flagrantly wrong or improper act to kill one or both of them without any legal consequence. That law remained in most states until the 1970s when women demanded equal killing rights. I promise, I'm not making this up.

I've never considered myself much of a fighter for women's rights. I was a lukewarm women's-libber in the 1960s, and these days I cringe at the word feminist because of the negative connotations. To be a feminist you have to have hairy legs and hate men, right? Wrong. And aren't feminists a bunch of raving radicals? Maybe. But they're also women like Harriet Tubman, Laura Ingalls Wilder, Rachel Carson, Rosa Parks, Erma Bombeck, and Jane Goodall.

Our First Feminist was Abigail Adams. Her strongest arguments through the years were for women's education. But she also asked her husband for protection from abuse. One famous letter to her husband John said, "I desire you would remember the ladies and be more generous and favorable to them than your ancestors. Do not put such unlimited power into the hands of husbands."

And Sojourner Truth was the Martin Luther King of feminists. Her famous speech was given in 1852 at the second annual convention of the women's rights movement in Akron, Ohio. "That man says that women need to be helped into carriages, and lifted over ditches, and to have the best place everywhere. Nobody ever helps me into carriages, or over mud puddles, or gives me any best places, and ain't I a woman? ... I have plowed, and planted, and gathered into barns, and no man could head me—and ain't I a woman? I have borne thirteen children and seen them most all sold off into slavery, and when I cried out with a mother's grief, none but Jesus heard—and ain't I a woman?"

I recently heard Rush Limbaugh, one of the great minds of the 15th Century, say that the only women's movement he cared about was watching a woman's rear end move when she walked. He went on to proclaim certain characteristics that were inherently feminine, as if there were genes for shopping, sewing and cooking.

Problem is, I would much rather spend time in a hardware store than in a dress boutique—and ain't I a woman? I'd rather toss a baseball than make a quilt—and ain't I a woman? I'd rather muck out a horse's stall than cook a casserole—and ain't I a woman? I'd rather drive a nail than thread a needle —and ain't I a woman?

I'm mighty glad there were American women who had the spunk and courage to stand up for the rest of us. Otherwise we might, like the women in Afghanistan, be totally without rights. Seems I take my rights for granted, but I shouldn't.

Happy Anniversary, women of America! Happy Anniversary to us.

Westward Women

It's time to salute women from our past. As I search for heroines, I have to ask, where are the great women of American lore, and why do we have to hunt so hard to find them? It's strange that the most consistent omission from the stories we treasure is the exclusion of the American woman.

When we think about the American Western frontier, it's easy to call to mind larger than life characters Daniel Boone, Davy Crocket, and Wild Bill Hickok. What about the common woman who went west with her children and belongings in a covered wagon?

Folks called the Wild West "no region for women." Anyone traveling westward wasn't likely to enjoy a painless journey. It was hard, lacking in almost all creature comforts. Death by drowning, fatal accidents from carelessly handled guns, and wagon mishaps were commonplace. There were hailstorms, tornadoes, blizzards, heat waves, floods, poisonous snakes and insect pestilence.

But have you heard about Margaret Reed? In July 1846, she reluctantly left her home in Illinois, with her husband James, their four children, and her ailing mother and set off for California. James promised that she would travel in unsurpassed luxury and style, with all her prized personal possessions. The covered wagon was two stories high, with a sleeping loft. It was outfitted with spring seats like the best stagecoaches, an iron stove, velvet curtains, and her cherished organ. Stocked with a six month supply of the best food and wine money could buy, the wagon pulled into formation with the rest of the Donner Party to head west.

The tragic story of the Donner Party is the most unforgettable tale of triumph and despair ever written in the history of the American West. Twenty five hundred miles away from home and only two days from safety, thirty-one men, women and children were stranded for an entire winter in the Sierra Nevada mountains by a succession of the worst blizzards on record. Out of provisions and starving, some members resorted to cannibalism in order to survive. Margaret and her children weren't among them. She kept them all alive on snow, bark, and leather broth until James, who had left the group to ride ahead seeking a rescue party, returned. The fact that her family didn't die—physically or spiritually—had absolutely nothing to do with the worldly goods she had counted on. They had abandoned the wagon and all it carried because it was too heavy and cumbersome to travel through the mountains. The possessions that saved Margaret and her children were her wits, faith, and courage.

The poignant diaries and journals of many other adventurous women who set off into the wilds, over the Rockies tell of journeys that were long, and hard, and unspeakably sad in places. When I dig deep into the past, I find scores of stories of tough women who reaffirm heart, grit, and cleverness that have nothing to do with gender.

The Joy of Eating

"One of the delights of life is eating
with friends; second to that is
talking about eating."

Laurie Colwin, *Home Cooking*

Baking Cakes

We sat sipping coffee from thick yellow mugs, greedily munching home-made coconut cake. And somebody said, "My mother used to make a delicious lemon-cheese cake."

"So did mine," I said. Suddenly I could almost taste the moist white layers, the creamy seven-minute icing, and the tangy yolk-colored lemon filling. And I rashly announced, "I'm gonna find Mother's recipe and make one."

It turned out getting the recipe wasn't all that easy. As I rummaged through my mother's old recipe box, I recalled asking her for the recipe years ago. "Where is it?" I'd groaned when she said she didn't have it.

"In my head somewhere," she apologized. "It was my mama's recipe and I don't think it was ever written down."

I wouldn't be dissuaded. I called my sister Jane. She didn't have it, but she joined the crusade and called our sister in South Carolina. "I have it," Beth said. And a few days later I received the neatly penned recipe in the mail with a note that said, "This is one of those old-fashioned recipes that takes a lot of stirring."

Back when my grandmother was keeping house in Eufaula in the early 1900s, cooking was definitely harder than it is these days. Since Grandmother Corbitt had twelve children, putting three meals on the table every day must have been a full-time job.

Grandpa owned a small store, so they had things other families didn't have. But they grew most of their food and cooked it on a wood stove.

They got their milk from a cow two times a day, and once a week they made butter. Grandmother did the milking herself. She wouldn't teach her seven daughters to milk the cow. "If you don't know how, you'll never have to do it," she told them.

On churning day she poured fresh milk into a round pan. After it sat for several hours the cream rose to the top, and a few hours later, it would sour and harden into clabber. Then the clabber was skimmed off and poured into a churn. The children liked to do the churning, because they could read while they pumped the dasher up and down. The day butter was churned the family had to drink the thin "skim milk" left at the bottom of the round pan. It had a sort of bluish tint, so they called it Blue John.

Fresh vegetables were picked from the half-acre garden, then washed and shelled, snapped, shucked or cut before they were cooked. The children gathered hens' eggs every day, but chopping off the chicken's head at frying time was another task Grandmother did herself.

On special occasions, a turkey from the store and a homegrown hog were cooked together outside in a big wash pot. Then the turkey was browned for about an hour in the oven. That made the outside crisp and the inside tender.

Grandmother's pear preserves were a family favorite, but making them was a 2-day chore. First the pears were picked, washed, peeled, cored, and sliced. Then she propped a ladder on two sawhorses, draped a sheet over the ladder, spread the pears on the sheet and left them out in the sun all day. At night, she took the pears inside and washed them, then put them in a big boiler in layers—a layer of pears, a layer of sugar, until all the pears were used. She sprinkled water on top so the pears would crystallize. The next morning they were ready to simmer for several hours. When the pears were tender and the syrup thick, she sealed them in sterilized wide-mouthed mason jars. She always cooked peach preserves with the peach on the seed, and she left the stems on her figs.

My grandmother made at least ten kinds of cakes, and they all took a lot of stirring. I still haven't gotten up the gumption to make her lemon-cheese cake. The only thing I've stirred lately is my morning cup of coffee.

Cultural Food

"What in tarnation is soul food?" I asked my sister Barbara who happens to be much more sophisticated and somewhat smarter than me. "It's what people who don't live in the south call Southern cooking," she explained. "It's what we call food."

That set me to pondering. You'd think food's food and eating's eating. It's just not so. The need to eat is biological, but the way we satisfy the need is cultural.

If you offer a piece of meat to a dog, there's no doubt he'll eat it. Offer the same meat to a person and he'll want to know: What kind is it? How big is it? How is it cooked? What is it served on? And what utensils will be provided?

I grew up so entrenched in the customs of the Deep South that it's sometimes hard for me to even consider that there are other ways. After all, who wouldn't want to eat bacon and fried eggs, toast slathered in butter and fig preserves, with plenty of orange juice and coffee to wash it down before heading out the back door for the day? And why would anyone balk about an ample noontime meal followed six hours later with a bountiful supper?

When I was a little girl, those 6 o'clock meals of meat loaf or salmon croquettes were complimented by steaming bowls of mashed potatoes, lots of fresh vegetables, and sugar-loaded ice tea. Supper ended with a different dessert every night.

But I know everybody doesn't eat that way. And it's not just the kinds of food; it's the way people eat. Some sit on the floor using their fingers, while others choose chairs and chopsticks.

My great-great grandmother's Creek Indian family kept a big pot of stew simmering over an open fire. A person ate when he was hungry—right out of the kettle with a shared spoon. The goulash was mushy and easy to chew, leading some anthropologists to figure that this method of cooking evolved into the Southern tradition of cooking vegetables until they're tender.

Most of my other forefathers came from across the puddle. I must have inherited a genetic trait for craving more than three meals a day from my British ancestors. The practice in England is to eat five times a day. There's the big breakfast followed by "elevenses"—coffee and scones at eleven. Then there's lunch, tea and crumpets at mid-afternoon, and dinner around seven. Sounds proper to me.

The Masai, a nomadic African tribe, raise cattle for a living. But their main source of food isn't beef. They prefer a liquid diet of cow's blood mixed with milk. And for a special treat, cow's urine is added to the blend. The brew ferments for a day or two until it's the consistency of soft cheese.

More than 1,000 kinds of insects are served routinely, cooked or still squirming, to folks throughout the world. Termites, beetle grubs, dragonflies, grasshoppers and crickets are munched on in places like Mexico, Thailand and Cambodia. Roasted, salted roaches are served as street fare in Bangkok.

I respect each person's right to chow down whenever, on whatever, with any utensil he might choose. As for me, I think I'll stick to my old habits.

Fried Chicken

I was thumbing through a *Southern Living* magazine in the dentist's office and came across a quote by Pulitzer Prize winning journalist Rick Bragg. He said, "I have never in my life gone to a restaurant and had fried chicken and been disappointed. Even bad fried chicken is better than no fried chicken at all. It's kinda like love."

Now as much as I hate to disagree with a Pulitzer Prize winner, I can't let a statement such as that go by unchallenged. Fact is, Bragg won acclaim for sports writing. He didn't even get honorable mention for fried chicken judging.

Of course, Bragg never tasted my mama's fried chicken. I know everybody in the world claims his own mama is the best cook who ever lived. But there's no way they can be right, because the thing is, my mama was the best cook ever to slap a meal on the table. And when it came to chicken, Daddy said, "If the Colonel could fry chicken like your mama, he'd be a general."

The only other person I've ever known who could come close to frying chicken like my mama was Joe Cameron, the long-time chef at Christchurch School in Virginia. Joe stopped off at the boys' boarding school looking for work in 1929. He was just passing through. They handed him an apron and chef's hat and he stayed on for forty-five years.

I moved to Christchurch in 1969 and was almost struck dumb when I tasted the food. This was no ordinary school cafeteria. This was soul food paradise. My biggest delight was that, like my mama, Joe could flat fry some chicken. Lightly salted and floured, the cut-up pieces were dropped in scalding fat and came out with thin, crisp skin on the outside and tender, juicy meat inside.

Faculty families were required to eat three meals a day in the dining hall. And we quickly learned that everything Joe Cameron cooked was scrumptious. We breakfasted on piles of scrambled eggs, bacon, sausage, biscuits, and strong-brewed coffee. During the mid-morning break we met in the lounge to scarf down soft sticky buns straight from the oven and more hot coffee. Lunch was homemade pizza or thick hamburgers and fries. Supper was a coat and tie affair every night. There were platters of meat, big bowls loaded with fresh vegetables, and rich, flaky desserts. In the five years I lived there I gained weight and lots of it.

Even the boys loved the food except for a few rare dishes. Scrapple, meat scraps and cornmeal seasoned with herbs and served sliced and fried, wasn't a favorite. Neither was a meal made of croquettes cooked in mounds standing straight up served with bowls of stewed tomato goulash. Faculty and students alike referred to that entrée as Anthills and Train Wreck. And there was Bug Juice, a mixture of fruit juices full of pulp that looked like gnats floating in a stagnant stream.

An 8x10 framed photo of a young Joe Cameron in his white chef's apron and puffy hat hangs in my study. Tall and lean, his skin the color of that pungent coffee only he could perk. When I knew Joe, he was older and rounder. The black hair, usually hidden beneath the tall hat, was graying. He was a kind, good-natured man with a soft smile. I said I'd leave Christchurch when Joe Cameron retired, and I did.

When I read Rick Bragg's statement that all fried chicken is tasty, I didn't know whether to laugh or cry. It jogged memories of my mama in the hot kitchen on North College Street and Joe Cameron in the inner sanctum of the Christchurch cookroom, and it made me drool worse than any of Pavlov's puppies.

Trust me, I'm not a finicky eater. I'm not at all persnickety. But when it comes to fried chicken, I'm just plain spoiled.

Living to Eat

The world is made up of two kinds of people—those who live to eat and those who eat to live. The latter group consists of what I call gastronomical Puritans, anti-cooks and Epicurean Philistines. Those who feel there's something sinful in nibbling culinary treats.

But I'm of a different persuasion—the living-to-eat kind. Fact is I'm so food-oriented my most cherished memories concern my taste buds. When I close my eyes and roam the neighborhood of my youth, it's not the great museums or the rousing adventures I recall. It's the dinky cafes and drive-thru restaurants that come to mind.

It's true. I've seen castles in Spain and strolled the streets of London and Paris. I've rafted Wyoming's Snake River and sailed the Chesapeake Bay. I've bumped along in San Francisco trolley cars, jigged to New Orleans jazz, and splashed in the waves at Waikiki. But when I reminisce, it's rarely those places I dream of. More often I dredge up visions of the Kopper Kettle, Mama's, the Bonanza Burger or the War Eagle Supper Club.

When I was a bouffant-haired teenager, the Kopper Kettle was nestled on the corner of Magnolia Avenue and Gay Street. I'd meet my friends there for a 10-cent burger or a hunk of coconut custard pie.

Around the bend on College Street hiding somewhere between J&M Bookstore and Ware's Jewelry was Mama's. Mama's was a small café that served homemade doughnuts and coffee. There were four booths with vinyl seats and thick oak tabletops.

We'd flip the partitions of the miniature wall-jukebox, pick a tune and drop a dime in the slot. Then we'd yell for Mama to top up our coffee and bring another warm doughnut plucked from the deep-fry-pot, laced with powdered-sugar icing.

Our favorite pastime was to pile in cars and cruise Opelika Road, checking out the new drive-ins. The Hungry Boy was the first drive-thru hamburger joint along that stretch of blacktop. And there was a Dairy-Delite where we ordered foot-long chilidogs and strawberry sundaes. But the Bonanza Burger was the hands-down best. Their double-burgers had finely shredded lettuce and a special secret sauce. For years I pursued the solution to the mystery of that tasty topping. Later I learned that it was just ordinary tarter sauce.

In the opposite direction, way out South College Street, was the War Eagle Supper Club. It was a crowded, dirty, noisy dive. But we went there for a good reason—pizza like no other. Truly spectacular thin-crust pizza studded with intricate patterns of pepperoni across a sea of spicy tomato sauce, topped with sprinkles of cheese. Each bite was chewy-crisp. While we waited, we munched pickled hard-boiled eggs that looked like a science fair experiment floating in gallon mayonnaise jars.

That was awhile ago—so far in the past that all-you-can-eat salad bars didn't exist. I suppose one day my grandchildren will get that faraway look and say, "Remember the calzones at Mellow Mushroom?" or "What I'd give for a turkey wrap at Amsterdam Cafe," or "I can still taste the Chicken Italians from Findley's Eatery."

And their children will roll their eyes and say, "Can somebody give us a ride to the Kudzu Kafé?"

Pantries

In my memories of long ago, most houses had a pantry off the kitchen. The kitchens were large and roomy workrooms, the heart of the home. Pantries were small, compact supply rooms the size of large walk-in closets, cul-de-sacs of rough hand-hewn pine shelves reinforced with an arsenal of home-canned fruits, vegetables and preserves.

A trip to the pantry meant crossing the wide expanse of a cozy kitchen filled with a cornucopia of fragrances, catching a whiff of sizzling bacon, sweet-smelling peaches waiting to be baked in deep-dish pies, and crisp-browned cinnamon toast coming out of the oven. On the back of the stove sat a big brown pot roast gently bubbling and a tea kettle heating up, its lid bumping up and down like a child on the back of a fat pony.

In one corner the smell of liquid starch and freshly pressed cotton lingered around the ironing board after a session with a flock of crisp little dresses and stiff white shirts. Nearby was the aroma of baby formula, fresh folded diapers, and talcum powder.

Over the porcelain sink, big windows let in light exposing the cluttered counter-tops. A rainbow of carrots, squash, and blood-red tomatoes sprawled in the sun like a gaggle of teenagers on the beach.

Pantry space was limited, so the delicacies stowed away in Mason jars were scrunched shoulder to shoulder—fig preserves, watermelon-rind pickles, and diced tomatoes. Other shelves held the staples—rice, rock salt, sugar, flour, and coffee.

When I consider my grandmother, who had only summer fruits and homegrown vegetables and could keep just carrots and turnips and potatoes fresh in the cellar, our age seems like something dreamed up by Jules Verne. Nowadays we can get strawberries in February, asparagus in March, peas in April, and oranges all the year around.

Our refrigerators hold frozen blueberries and broccoli and jugs of factory-squeezed orange juice. Rows of canned soup, sliced bread, and Smucker's Jelly sit on our fake-wood shelves.

Scrubbed Formica counter tops are edged with a battery of electric toasters, coffee makers, and half a dozen other automatic gadgets, including a microwave oven. Our generation of anti-cooks emphasizes specialty doodads and shelves of cookbooks unspotted by use. Kitchens have become showrooms with ruffled curtains over the chrome sink. The color of the stove matches the wallpaper and there are rows of spice bottles in a mahogany rack. Copper-bottomed pots and pans hang from hooks. I can imagine the cook in her fluffy housecoat pouring boiling water into instant coffee.

The modern kitchen has become a place of beauty rather than a work-place. Out of immaculate ovens will never come a soufflé or a loaf of home-made bread. These bright cubicles are no longer the heart of the home, not rooms to live in but places to get away from.

If you ever come across a real kitchen, you'll know it by its fragrances and clutter—a jumble of fruit rinds, piecrust shavings, egg-spotted bowls, untidy beaters, unwashed serving spoons, vegetable scrapings; the whole stove occupied with things stewing, simmering, blanching, sautéing, bub-bling in pots. It won't be neat. It won't be fancy. But there'll be something sweet-smelling twirling in a bowl and something savory baking in the oven. And of course, there'll be a well-stocked pantry nearby.

Supper

For years I ate supper. Supper was sometime between five o'clock and six, and the whole family showed up at the table on time to eat. I lived in the Deep South then.

Later I moved north to Virginia, and it didn't take me long to realize I'd moved into another world—the world of dinner eaters. Until then, in my experience, dinner was eaten only once a week, always at 12:30 on Sunday afternoon after church. Dinner was eaten in the dining room around the big walnut table that was draped with a freshly washed white linen tablecloth. There were matching cloth napkins, silver eating utensils, and bone china plates.

Sunday dinner was fried chicken or pot roast with rice and gravy that Mama put on the table while I read the funny papers. There were china bowls filled with vegetables, and a silver-plate basket stuffed with tiny buttered rolls. We all drank cold sweet tea served in icy crystal goblets.

We ate supper in the kitchen at a smaller, uncovered table. And the menu consisted of simpler fare, casseroles that would fill up a family of seven—corned beef hash, tuna casserole or American chop suey. We dug into hot bowls of mashed potatoes, and spooned out scoops of juicy slaw or apple and carrot salad. Fried corn bread was the supper bread. Mama had a big blue ceramic pitcher for brewing tea every day. At suppertime the pitcher sat in the middle of the table, and the grown-ups drank tea from jelly glasses. Seems all our meals, whether dinner or supper, ended with a generous slab of cake.

We ate supper between five and six even when we were on the road. When my oldest sister won a Fulbright Scholarship to Austria, we piled in the Ford and drove her to New York City to catch the boat. Daddy thought it would be a good experience for us to eat at the Stork Club, so the family filed in at 5:15 for supper.

We couldn't understand why we were the only ones there to eat or why the waiters were still setting the tables. Of course that night out on the town didn't change our way of doing things. I kept right on eating supper—until I moved.

Even though you might not think Virginia is exactly a northern territory, I'm here to tell you that those people ate dinner every night of the week and didn't think a thing about it. And after living there for only five short years, I came back home thinking dinner was at 6:30 at night, lunch was at midday, and supper had disappeared from the face of the earth.

There was a short transition period in which I remained a closet dinner eater. But sometimes I'd let it slip out. "What time are we eating dinner?" I asked my sister when she invited me over.

"Supper will be at 5:30," she said. "Or as soon as I get the corn bread fried."

It didn't take me long to reacclimate. And I've been a supper eater ever since. Every night of the week, every week of the year, for years and years, without fail.

The Great Outdoors

"I love being outdoors, love taking
a long walk with my dogs and
looking at trees, flowers, the sky."

Audrey Hepburn

Chattahoochee River

On cold, rainy mornings, lying hunkered down in my toast-warm bed I think about how pleasant it will be when it's spring and mild, sunny days return. Rolling over on my lumpy pillow, I focus on warm-weather pastime, like skipping smooth stones across the soft, warm surface of a lazy river. And I catch myself humming a few bars of "Cruising Down the River On A Sunday Afternoon."

A hundred-and-fifty years ago the main roads were rivers. Steamboats, barges, paddleboats and pontoons serpentined their way up and down rivers on a regular basis. Nowadays it's a novelty to see a riverboat churning along, and most of us wouldn't consider traveling the inland waterways.

As a child the only river I knew on a first-name basis was the slow-moving Chattahoochee. On the night I was born this placid river exploded, flooding my birthplace, the little town of West Point, Georgia. My sisters remember neighbors paddling square-ended johnboats and narrow-nosed canoes around town. As far as I know that's the only time the river's mud-brown water spilled over its banks.

The laid-back Chattahoochee carved its way through the center of West Point. My family's house was on the same side as the Methodist Church and the school. But if we wanted to go downtown to a movie, the library, or the stores we had to cross the steel-and-concrete bridge.

Across the river, on the Alabama side, my daddy built a rock cabin on a bluff overlooking the Chattahoochee River. That's where I spent most of my childhood weekends and summer vacations. My sister Jane and I ran along the banks jumping over moccasin holes, climbing in and out of an old rowboat that was tied to a tree stump, "playing like" we were Creek Indians who once inhabited those piney woods. We didn't know that the name "Chattahoochee" comes from a Creek Indian word meaning "pictured rock."

Sometimes Daddy would row us out in the boat and we'd hemstitch our way along the low-lying land to a small cave that jutted out at the tip of the bluff. Legend had it that this was an old Indian cave called "Dover's Den." I dreamed of exploring the cavern searching for artifacts, but Daddy said there'd be whole families of moccasins living there. So I mostly just sat on top of the overhang and was comforted by the constant flowing of the gentle water.

One thing we never did was fish. Daddy always said he'd take me when conditions were right. Seems it was always too windy or too still, or the water was too muddy, too clear, too hot or too cold.

The Chattahoochee is a remarkable river. Rising in the Blue Ridge Mountains, it follows the general slope of the land flowing south to form half the boundary between Georgia and Alabama. Farther south, it joins the Flint River and flows into the Gulf.

Today reckless dumping of sewage and toxic industrial waste is poisoning the river. I had nothing to do with the pollution of the Chattahoochee, but I'm sad and ashamed. Most folks I know feel the same. And those who thoughtlessly participated in making the Chattahoochee one of the most endangered rivers in the U.S.—they must be the most ashamed of all.

Chewacla

The Appalachian Mountains roll and tumble down the continent for 1,500 miles, then fade like the rushing ripple of a distant splash on a hill called Chewacla.

Most folks don't have a clue that Chewacla State Park occupies one of the last hills in the ancient Appalachian chain, or that it's the southwestern tip of Pine Mountain in Georgia. I found out a few facts about the park's various rocks and formations a while back when I chaperoned a middle-school field trip. I learned that Chewacla's geological variety, including the scenic waterfalls, is attributed to its location on the fall line, which separates the Piedmont plateau from the lower coastal plain. "There's a lot of relief at Chewacla," an Auburn University geologist, told us. To geologists, relief is a change in elevation. To others, it's a change in altitude.

The 696-acre park was established in the 1930s as a work camp for the Civilian Conservation Corps. The CCC built the park's cabins and pavilions from stone cut from the earth nearby. Those same workers built the dam on Moore's Mill Creek and flooded the 26-acre Chewacla Lake.

It's been said that Chewacla is the best-kept secret in East Alabama. That may be true, but I've known about the park almost all my life. When I was a little girl, Chewacla was a favorite hangout for the Auburn crowd.

Church groups gathered at the pavilion on top of the "mountain" for Sunday afternoon picnics and softball games or to watch the sun come up on Easter morning. Families met to enjoy the playground and hike the narrow pine-straw trails. Fishermen wiled away lazy afternoons in flat-bottomed boats floating on the lake stocked with bass, crappie, bream, and catfish. And Girls Scouts built campfires in the thickets, roasting marshmallows over leaping flames. When the soft confections were toasted, they were stuffed with Hershey bars between Graham crackers to make S'Mores.

As a teenager I joined friends to swim in the lake. We spread colorful beach towels on the sandy shore and "lay out" to catch some rays. When we felt parched, we'd jump in the chilly water. We didn't know and probably didn't care that the reason the water was so pleasant was because it flowed from an artesian spring near the diving platform, keeping the temperature a cool 65 degrees even in August.

When I was an Auburn University student, Chewacla was a favorite spot for cheap dates, wet romps in the waterfalls, or laid-back afternoons gazing at textbooks. Later as a young mother, I started the process over with my own children. And now I'm beginning to do it all again with another generation of children.

If it weren't for the distant groaning of tractors and trucks cranking up in the quarry nearby, it would be easy to imagine Chewacla's hills farther north in the middle of the Smokey Mountains. The placid scenery hides the park's nagging environmental problems, but those droning sounds are reminders that Chewacla is plagued with the pains of development.

Moore's Mill Creek, which flows through the heart of Auburn's new neighborhoods, was once deep and wide as it spilled into Chewacla Lake. Today the creek is choked with silt and Chewacla Lake is slowly filling with sand. At its deepest point, the lake measures just 22 feet. It's not likely that the silt will ever be dredged from the lake because heavy equipment needed for the job would destroy the park's steep hillsides.

Could be that the best-kept secret isn't the park itself, but the insidious desecration of the sanctuary.

Conservation

"If I start now?" my daughter used to ask when I warned her of some impending doom. It would begin with my motherly admonishing, "If you don't brush your teeth twice a day, your teeth are going to fall out." That was followed by her panic stricken, "If I start now?" And I assured her, "Yes, it'll be all right if you start now."

I think of that as I worry about the future. And there's no doubt in my mind that if we don't start changing our ways, we're in for trouble.

This isn't anything new. About 9,000 years ago the Natufians settled down near modern day Amman, Jordan. As archaeologists uncovered this Neolithic village, they found homes with manmade white plaster floors. It takes loads of wood to roast stone that is ground into powder to make the material they were so fond of. Later, the Natufians abandoned their village, because they had over-exploited their natural environment, using up the trees.

I've done my share of ranting about leveling 200-year-old trees in Auburn. I've griped that as we expand our borders, the chirping of redbirds has been replaced by the snarl of bulldozers chewing up the land. But it's not just birds that pay a price for human chopping, leveling, and poisoning.

When biologist, Rachel Carson, got a letter expressing concern about pesticides being sprayed over a bird sanctuary, she spent four years researching and writing "Silent Spring." The book explained how life-forms are interrelated and how poisons we use to kill insects seep through the food chain to contaminate humans. When it was published in 1962, the chemical industry viciously attacked Carson, calling the book "science fiction." *Time* called it an "emotional outburst." *Reader's Digest* canceled a contract to condense the book. And a Federal Pest Control Board member said, "I thought she was a spinster. What's she so worried about genetics for?"

Then scientists, stimulated by Carson's work, started finding DDT in human milk. Now all pesticides have to be approved by the Environmental Protection Agency. But many received "grand-fathered" okays, and in 1992, the EPA stopped requiring most testing before approval of new pesticides.

Most of us feel helpless to change the course of environmental destruction. But I'm convinced a little awareness, especially educating children, goes a long way. I overheard a fourth-grader say, "I like to play indoors, 'cause that's where all the electrical outlets are." He has no idea what he's missing. Jennifer Lolley, the administrator of Auburn's Forest Ecology Preserve, is active in getting kids into the woods. During the school year, she has afternoon trail hikes. Saturday mornings there are programs about bats, spiders, and snakes. Chinaberry trees and honeysuckle vines. When school's out, there's summer camp for daylong, hands-on study of plants and critters.

Rachel Carson said, "Conservation is a cause that has no end. There is no point at which we say, 'Our work is finished.'"

It seems we've hardly begun. But maybe if we start now...just maybe.

Save the Rivers

At the end of the Ice Age when the glaciers melted, water changed the face of the earth. People started settling down, and when they did, they lived by rivers. The dugout canoe was invented, and for centuries the main roads were rivers.

When I close my eyes and mosey through the neighborhood of my childhood, the Chattahoochee River runs through it. As a little girl, that was the only river I could call by name. Way before I could tie my shoes, my family bought a piece of piney woods on an Alabama bluff overlooking the nut-brown waterway. Daddy built a five-room rock cabin there, our hide-away on weekends and summer vacations.

I spent those days running barefoot along the fertile riverbank, in the sanctuary of the thicket, coming out only at the urgent calling of an adult. I squished my toes in the rusty-red mud and skipped flat stones across the glassy water. At sunset I'd sit on a granite overhang and gaze at the laid-back river moving slowly toward the Gulf of Mexico.

It was quiet there, and peaceful in that Creek Indian country. I watched the still water as if I were enjoying a Monet landscape. I took in mockingbirds scolding corn snakes that dangled from pine branches; heard the chirrup of crickets camouflaged in the brambled blackberry bushes.

Back then, I thought all rivers were alike. Sort of muddy, lazy bodies of freshwater. That was before I moved to the Tidewater area of Virginia and lived on a knob of hill that looked out on the Rappahannock River; before my crash course in the joys of a different kind of river, one filled with swells and waves as the brackish water rose and fell with the tides. Flowing toward the Atlantic, the fickle gray-green water could turn from smooth and easygoing to choppy and turbulent with a stiff nor'Easter blowing up a squall.

I bought an old 20-foot Indian Landing day-sailer, and learned to navigate the wooden sloop in the wake of hoarse honking oyster boats; to the sweet, raspy "eeee! eeee!" of gulls dipping and soaring over the shoreline. I'd tack my way along the sandy shore through patches of sharp smelling seaweed, then jibe and race toward the Chesapeake Bay on a broad reach.

In the cool of sundown, we'd stroll to the end of the weatherworn dock armed with crab nets. Using a raw chicken neck as bait, it didn't take long to fill a bucket with hard and soft-shell crabs.

I can't think of much my two rivers have in common except both are in crisis. The 70 miles of Chattahoochee from Atlanta to West Point is among the five most polluted stretches of river in the nation. And in Urbanna, Virginia, the local Fall Oyster Festival stays alive by shipping in oysters from Florida.

There's an Alabama/Georgia group trying to "SAVE THE HOOCH!" and a similar one in Virginia to "SAVE THE RIVAH!" I hope it isn't too late.

Yellowstone

Truth is stranger than fiction. Twentieth Century novels had us thinking that by now we'd be shuttling from one space station to the next to visit friends. And we'd be wearing disposable clothes that looked like shiny snakeskin snorkeling suits. Of course everyone would be svelte because the only nourishment would come from capsules.

No science fiction that I read predicted computers, DVDs, answering machines, cell phones, MRIs, organ transplants, microwaves, faxes or digital cable. They sure didn't mention the fact that when you went on a vacation you'd mostly find mass people and concrete.

Lucky for us, explorers saw what was coming and promoted the idea of national parks. "Out thar in the Yellowstone," Jim Bridger related, "thar's a river that flows so fast it gets hot on the bottom." Congressmen listened to Bridger's stories and made Yellowstone the first national park in 1872. Back then the parks were called "pleasuring grounds." Congress set up the National Park Service in 1916.

I've camped in dozens of national parks over the years. From Shenandoah and Great Smoky Mountain in the southeast to Grand Canyon and Death Valley in the southwest to Rocky Mountain, Grand Teton, Yellowstone, and Crater Lake in the west. My brother-in-law kindled my enthusiasm for these scenic sanctuaries. And I agree with the National Geographic Society that the parks "strengthen bodies, refresh minds, uplift spirit, and enrich leisure."

I shudder to think what our country would be like without the parks. In our national frenzy to blacktop the earth and make a fast buck, I'm afraid the splendor of the wilderness would be long lost. As it is, bulldozers have crept like fungus closer and closer to land adjacent to the parks and have turned nearby villages into so many tinsel towns.

I remember my first trip to the Grand Teton National Park as a 13-year-old. We camped at Jenny Lake for two weeks, and during that venture we went into the hamlet of Jackson Hole a couple of times. Jackson Hole consisted of a dirt road and a handful of shops.

A few summers ago I camped at Jenny Lake again. It hadn't changed much. But I didn't recognize Jackson Hole. It was just another tourist trap with rows of expensive shops and restaurants. Seems it's that way everywhere. Outside Rocky Mountain National Park is Estes Park. Sounds rustic, but it's only more stores and eateries. And Smoky Mountain National Park has Pigeon Forge with its motels and outlet malls pressing against its boundaries.

The Park Service has grown to 368 units covering roughly 80 millio
square miles. The annual budget is about $972 million, and visitor fees brin
in about $100 million a year.

There's been talk of closing parks. Two Smoky Mountain campground
have been closed and Yosemite's potholed roads haven't been mended. Dam
age and debris from storms won't be cleaned up in many parks. And ther
will be fewer rangers.

As Congress fights to shut down parks, imagine pitching a tent and eat
ing s'mores by a crackling campfire. Picture yourself canoeing, fishing, hik
ing, watching elk graze or trumpeter swans swim in a quiet, out-of-the-wa
oasis.

If our parklands aren't protected, imagine yourself waiting in a long lin
on hot asphalt at an amusement park whining, "Are we having fun yet?"

For What It's Worth

"People can tell you to keep your
mouth shut, but that doesn't keep
you from having your own opinion."

Anne Frank, *The Diary of a Young Girl*

All I Need to Know

All I really need to know I learned at 318 North College Street. The years I lived in that two-story, white columned house across from the railroad tracks were formative years. Ages 7 to 13. That's the time spent watching others, figuring out what life is all about. Here's what I learned:

*Money can buy stuff, but not memories. Raising five children without credit cards wasn't easy. We didn't have a bunch of material goods, but we have plenty of stories to tell.

*Be willing to fight for what's important. Late one night a massive man staggered to our door waving a broken whiskey bottle. My daddy, who was 5'6" with his shoes on, went after the drunk barehanded. The man fled, feet slapping the pavement for all he was worth.

*It's an overactive fork, not an underactive metabolism that causes a person to be overweight.

*Good people and bad people are found in each race, gender, ethnic group, and social class.

*You learn a lot perched unseen in the arms of a dogwood tree on the corner of North College and Mitcham Avenue.

*Life is much more fun if you can play a musical instrument.

*Open your home to those who need a place to stay. Several college students lived with us, including Tong, a Korean girl. And Helga, the German girl who thought she was paying. But our only pay was having them become part of our family for a time.

*Never point a gun at another person—not even a toy gun.

*Hearing a train whistle at night while you're in bed can stir the imagination like nothing else can.

*Very important people are just like anybody else only sometimes nicer. Paul Shields Haley of Haley Center fame and U.S. Senator John Sparkman were regulars at our house. They were in the nicer category.

*Have a pet—especially a dog. No matter how you look, they're always glad to see you. And they don't talk back.

*You have to do some things you don't feel like doing, like emptying the litter box and scrubbing the bathtub.

*Be satisfied with who you are. My aunt said that if I could kiss my elbow I'd turn into a boy. I strained for years, but when I turned 12, I was glad I had short lips.

*It's important to get a good education. All those students coming and going made an impression after a while.

*Laughter really is the best medicine. My mother and her six sisters taught me to find humor in life. My daddy showed me how to laugh at myself.

*Remember the Sabbath.

*Walking is more fun if you're going somewhere. Living close to town, we didn't have to walk for exercise. We walked wherever we went.

*Handicapped people can be the most capable of all.

*Television will never replace reading.

*Enjoy the small everyday things. Don't wait for a trip to Paris.

*Conversation around the kitchen table is more important than a summit conference. That's where such things as dreams, ideas, possessions, love, and promises are discussed.

I forgot many of these things along the way and had to relearn them, but I won't forget again. I hope.

Behind the Wheel

When I turned 16, my daddy gave me a set of keys to his blue Ford Galaxy. The fact that I had a wreck the next day didn't seem to discourage him in the least. In fact, he shocked me by saying, "I'm just glad nobody got hurt."

When my 18th birthday rolled around, he bought me a brand spanking new lime-sherbet-green VW Beetle of my very own. I figured carrying the keys to that aluminum bubble on wheels was a proud symbol of my new-found adulthood. A rite of passage to independence. And I zoomed through high cotton with different sets of car keys for the next 30-something years.

Then Daddy reached the time in his life when his reflexes weren't quite so good, and his eyes were even worse. My sisters and I knew he shouldn't drive anymore. When he started having minor accidents, I found myself saying the same thing he'd said to me when I was a teenager, "I'm just glad nobody got hurt."

But even though we constantly worried that the next time might be more serious, there was no Dr. Spock for the middle-aged daughters of an elderly father. There was nothing spelled out, or any set rules on how to take care of an aging father, to watch out for him and, at the same time, respect his independence.

Finally, the doctor told us that Daddy absolutely could not drive anymore. "You'll have to tell him," he said. "I can't tell the man he has to hand over his car keys."

So the task of key removal fell to the daughters. We took his keys, and his life was never the same. In giving up his place in the driver's seat, he had made the final passage into old age. The passage to dependence.

The other day a friend told me that her 92-year-old mother-in-law still drives from Gadsden, AL to Atlanta to visit. Her trip includes changing lanes on I-75 and I-285. And although I consider driving one of my better skills, I find myself peeking around the corner of two or three decades wondering what I'll want and what I'll do. It seems the next move in the ongoing saga, the give and take of car keys, will involve me giving or my daughter taking.

And I wonder if my baby girl's middle-age years will be full of worries about me. Will she lose sleep over how to ease me out of the driver's seat? Will she be able to avoid being overbearing or neglectful?

My mother had the good sense at an early age to put her car keys in a drawer and announce to the family that she didn't want to drive anymore. And she never did. Ever.

I hope I'll have the grace to navigate that next turn in the road with as much wisdom and become a perfect passenger.

Cornerstone

I can barely remember when I was a tiny girl with bobbed hair and baby teeth. But one thing that stands firm in my mind is the building of the family cabin. Daddy bought a few acres of piney-woods on a bluff overlooking the Chattahoochee River and for thirty years we worked, played, and rested there.

The first ten years were the building years. On trips with Mama and Daddy, my sister Jane and I were stationed at the back windows as lookouts for pretty stones on the side of the road. We'd yell, "There's one!" And Daddy would screech to a stop, back up, and heave the treasure into the car-trunk.

On Saturdays we mixed thick gray cement, half-bags at a time, and Daddy did rockwork while he listened to out-of-town Auburn football games. Years later we'd spot a bump in a row of stone steps and laugh, remembering that he'd built the stairs as he listened to a nerve wracking Auburn-Georgia Tech game.

Once the original four-room cabin was complete, it became the meeting place for church youth groups and family get-togethers. Every summer my mother and her six sisters spent a week there resting and relaxing, reading and eating, talking and laughing. At the end of the week, the rest of the Corbitt clan showed up for the annual family reunion.

Daddy built a one-room rock house with electricity for Jane and me. We called it the "dollhouse" and we spent long hours there. It was in the dollhouse, on hot summer days, that I discovered the joy of reading. Sprawled on a bed with a droning, plug-in fan stirring up the humid air, I greedily flipped pages that took me other places while our little black dog dozed at my feet.

We begged Daddy to build us a swimming pool and he always said, "If you'll dig the hole, I'll build it." So one summer morning after he'd gone to Atlanta on business for the day, Jane convinced the man Daddy had hired to do yard work to spend the whole day digging. When Daddy drove up at sundown and saw that there was a gigantic hole and realized he'd paid the man to dig it, he shook his head and laughed. He knew he'd been outsmarted. We got our pool, and we'd stay in it until our skin was as brown and wrinkled as a dried fig, and Mama made us get out.

My best memories of childhood come from those times at the cabin. Breakfast-time in the kitchen was the only cool part of a summer day. I recall the feel of that damp early-morning air on my face, sniffing the sweet smell of pine mixed with sizzling bacon, the happy songs of waking-up birds, and the eerie image of a black racer hanging from a tall tree branch.

I often stood barefoot as a child on a summer evening watching the yellow and white festoons of honey suckle against the rails of the wrap-around porch. And I felt a deep affection for every stick and stone of the place.

But I grew up and found that it was more than the rocks and two-by-fours, more than the cement and sand. It even goes beyond the time spent enjoying the finished product. I conjure up a vision of my family silhouetted against the sunlight rippling on the river—my laughing, arguing, working family. And I think – that's what it's all about. Building a family. That's what lasts when the rest of it is all over. The cornerstone—your family.

Libraries

When I was a little girl we rarely spent hard-earned cash on new books. But that wasn't a major problem because there was a lending library nearby.

My best memory of early childhood in West Point, Georgia is of weekly trips to that library. We'd walk, or sometimes drive, across the Chattahoochee River Bridge to the tiny red-brick building, and while Mother browsed the big people's shelves, my chubby fingers flipped the pages of picture books.

The library lady sat in a wheelchair behind the desk shuffling Library of Congress cards, ready to punch the due date on books. Stamp. A book slammed. Stamp. The next book. It didn't matter that I couldn't read or that I wasn't supposed to laugh or talk out loud, the trip to the library was my favorite adventure. Back home my sisters sprawled in squashy chairs turning the pages of their borrowed books lickety-split while I sat in my little red rocker reading my books upside-down.

When my family moved to Auburn in the fifties, we all got library cards at the Hollifield Public Library on North Gay Street. The first chapter-book I ever read, a biography of Lou Gehrig, came from those shelves. And when I was sick, Mother brought home *Little Men*, *The Hardy Boys*, and the Eleanor Estes *Moffat* series and read aloud to me.

I left Auburn after I finished college. But I found new libraries wherever I went. In Atlanta, I borrowed books from the scholarly stacks of the four-floor Asa Griggs Candler Library at Emory University. I was enchanted by that dignified structure with its spiral staircases and floor to ceiling publications

And later when I lived in tidewater Virginia, I frequented the quaint library that perched on a knoll overlooking Urbanna Harbor. Steep stairs led to the brick cottage that was originally a tobacco warehouse built in 1766. It consisted of one large room, neatly bisected by the checkout desk. To the right and left, reading material was arranged alphabetically on hand-hewn hardwood shelves by an all-volunteer staff.

Back in Auburn the Hollifield Library had moved to a bigger, newer, more modern building on Ross Street, and for years I went there on a regular basis. The out-of-date subject-author-title cards stuffed in wooden drawers had been replaced by computers that were so simple even I could use them. And thanks to the Auburn Lions Club there was a growing section of large-print books and books on tape. As we might have predicted, the building soon became too cramped and there wasn't enough space for new material. So the city bought the old Lakeview Baptist Church property on Dean Road and again built a bigger, newer, more modern library.

On a recent trip to Columbia, South Carolina I visited the Richland County Library. This shiny new downtown structure has been ranked 21st out of 404 urban public libraries in the nation, ahead of Boston and New York City. And it's tops in the Southeast.

I was enthralled with this high-tech, glass-walled edifice. The main floor is a sea of fiction and non-fiction with a large-print section bigger than some libraries I've seen. The center is an island of easy-to-use computers, and escalators glide silently upstairs.

But best of all is the basement—a children's paradise. The walls are painted with giant pictures from Sendak's colorful *Where The Wild Things Are*, and long-limbed potted plants add to the jungle aura. Tables are topped with puzzles and games and kid-friendly computers while snuggly chairs and stuffed animals entice the tiny tots.

Wherever I go, I like to explore the library. Once inside, I'm home.

Secondhand Bookstores

Sifting through the layers of my past, I recall diversions that have made a difference in the trajectory of my life. My christening into the world of used bookstores came when I was seventeen, visiting my sister in Kentucky. She handed me the keys to the VW and a Lexington city-map with the location of a secondhand bookstore circled. So with the top down and the radio blaring, I steered the Bug through a grid of unfamiliar streets and somehow found my introduction to secular-heaven. I still recall that one-room cottage set back from the road. As I walked the aisles of that bookshop, I found all the great writers from Jane Austen to Emile Zola. Each book, hard-bound and paperback alike, cost a dime apiece, so I filled a brown bag and read them blissfully one at time. When I look at my bookshelves today, I spot tattered copies of editions that came from those hand-hewn shelves. *The Sound and the Fury, The Human Comedy, Wuthering Heights,* and *Cannery Row.* Now the pages are yellow and brittle, the covers hanging on with ecru tape.

Years later when I was a graduate student in Atlanta, I found another used-book store by accident while exploring a neighborhood a half-mile from my Ponce de Leon apartment. I've long forgotten the name, but that was before bookstores had clever names. I think that dumpy, smoke-filled establishment merely had a shabby sign that said, "Books." I never ventured past the front where there were rows of serious literature. In the back there was a room closed off by a curtain. Sleazy looking men headed to that section, and I knew they were in an area of what we called "dirty" books. It gave me the creeps, but I figured they had their section and I had mine. And before long I was immersed in a dreamland of fiction. I took that same walk for months. Each time I'd hesitate at the door, then plunge in like Dorothy dropping into Oz. I stocked up on more classics—Hemingway, Scott Fitzgerald, Dostoyevsky, and Henry James. I've kept those books too. The crackling pages and tattered covers, much like the stuffed bunny in "The Velveteen Rabbit," they've been loved almost beyond recognition.

I still search for out-of-the-way bookstores wherever I go, places called Cup and Chaucer and Bookworm. All book lovers have a favorite store. Mine is The Gnu's Room right here in Auburn. I duck inside, rifle the shelves and nose through unknown novels. I feast on the titles and the art on the dust jackets.

The voice of doom tells us there'll soon be no more printed books on shelves. We're not threatened by the frightening vision of the future in *Fahrenheit 451* where firemen burn the books. It's Kindles, Nooks and iPads we fear. Already, Borders and a number of independent bookstores are gone forever. But I believe there will always be enough "hard copy" book lovers left to keep out-of-the-way used-book stores around.

Southern Childhood

On muggy afternoons I like to daydream—traipse through the old stomping grounds of my childhood and reminisce about summers past.

Used to be summertime was the best time of the year. In the summer the rules were suspended; there was no set time to go to bed.

Mama would start calling us in around a quarter till dark, and we'd beg, "Just five more minutes!"

Our twilight games were simple. Chasing lightning bugs and practicing sliding into second on a thick bib of zoysia grass in the corner of the yard.

It was cooler outside at dusk than in the house. Inside, big oscillating fans droned, struggling to stir the sluggish air. Adults sat outside on porches pushing the air with hand-held cardboard fans that advertised some hardware store. The other hand slapped at mosquitoes.

Whenever I hurried inside for a drink of water, Mama would holler, "Don't let the screen door slam!" And I'd reach back too late to stop the bang.

After a rain there was a lingering hint of honeysuckle and gardenia perfume in the air. Gardenias were strictly for sniffing; honeysuckle offered an added treat. I'd pluck a yellow blossom from the vine, breaking off the tip, and pulling the string out to enjoy the drop of nectar as it hit my tongue.

When I gathered fat blackberries, I'd eat as I picked, but I knew they'd taste sweeter in the deep-dish pie Mama would bake for supper. Since I was the baby of the family, Mama reluctantly allowed me to sit on the counter dangling my bare feet and watch her roll the dough on a slab of wood. Her rolling pin was missing a handle, but that didn't slow her down. When the crust was as thin as a penny postcard, she'd cut it in strips and arrange them like a tic-tac-toe grid over the stewed sugary berries in a pan.

Food was always a big part of my Southern childhood, but certain foods could only be had in the summer. Tender red tomatoes peeled, sliced, salted and piled on soft white bread slathered in real mayonnaise. A five star chef couldn't come up with a recipe that tasty. Big bowls of fresh vegetables. Heavy watermelons so juicy they had to be eaten outdoors with the sticky liquid dripping from elbows and chins, and the seeds spit into the bushes. And, of course, hand-churned ice cream.

Turns out I'm thankful for growing up Southern. When I see droves of people migrating from the four corners of the world, I want to say, "Don't! It's too hot and humid. The vermin are awful. We're infested with snakes, spiders, roaches, red bugs and skeeters. Nobody wears shoes, and we talk funny.

We can let the truth be our little secret.

Suppose You Had No Nose

It's frustrating to take my little gray-bearded Schnauzer to walk. She has to stop every thirty seconds to pick up a scent. Aardvark-like she noses around the familiar neighborhood sniffing indiscriminately—garbage, flowers, people, and bugs. She can't help it. Schnauzers were bred to "go to ground," smelling out vermin. Still, I'm struck by the way she uses her nose to make her way through the well-known streets.

Compared to dogs, humans have a puny sense of smell. Even so, odors have a powerful impact on us. Scents bring back vivid memories of people and places. "Smell," said Helen Keller, "is a potent wizard that transports us across thousands of miles and all the years we have lived."

Some of the first smells I remember were far back in my childhood, soon after I learned to walk. Seems our kitchen was always filled with the aroma of pot roasts bubbling, fried chicken sizzling, gingerbread rising in the oven, or chopped up boiled eggs and Kraft mayonnaise being stirred into potato salad.

My three unmarried aunts were retired nurses who had practiced in the days before penicillin; times when people died from simple wounds that became infected, when soap and disinfectants were an arsenal against disease. The sterile smell of cleansers hung in the air throughout their square clapboard house. Occasionally when I'm washing clothes or scrubbing the bathtub, my nose fills with the scent of soapsuds, and suddenly, with no warning, I'll be transported for a moment to their white cottage on a hill.

And one whiff of a gardenia blossom takes me to the back porch of that same bungalow where a river of gardenia bushes hugged the stoop. The perfume from those shrubs was so sweet it engulfed me, making me swimmy-headed.

I'm partial to all kinds of smells from a sweaty horse to puppy-breath to a baby fresh out of a bath. I like the distinct oregano and onion odor that hits me when I step into an Italian restaurant. And I'm drawn to the fruity fragrance of pipe tobacco.

Psychologist Robert Baron staged an experiment to see if the heady aroma of coffee or the soothing smell of baking cookies might lull people into acts of kindness. As consumers strolled past Cinnabon and Banana Republic in the climate-controlled, color-coordinated corridors of a mall in upstate New York, they met young folks requesting change for a dollar. Little did the subjects suspect that their conduct was being evaluated. Turned out that while under the olfactory influence of roasting coffee or baking cookie dough, people were more than twice as likely to provide a stranger with change for a dollar than they were in unscented surroundings. Baron concluded, "Good fragrances make people happy. And when people feel happy, they're nicer to one another."

The opposite is true too. Craig Anderson of the University of Missouri says, "Unpleasant smells can make people aggressive by putting them in bad moods."

Bad smells also bring back memories. Not long ago my grandbuddy DJ and I walked into a building that had just been scoured with a strong-smelling disinfectant. "This place smells like the Birmingham bus station bathroom," I blurted out. He laughed and asked me, "Have you ever been in that place?" I told him that, unfortunately, I had.

But bad smells can trigger good memories. The awful odor of rotten seaweed and dead fish takes me happily to the banks of the Rappahannock River in Virginia. And one sniff of a mildewed canvas tent shifts me to the foot of Mt. Teewinot in Wyoming's Grand Tetons.

Fact is, almost everything that comes from my imagination, emotions, or observation filters first through my nose.

Where Were You?

The Big Bang. The Apocalypse. Auburn, Alabama, January 15, 1978. Heavy-eyed Sunday morning sleepers awakened shortly after 8 a.m. to the startling news that much of downtown Auburn had been ripped apart by a natural gas explosion. The report of the blast made the national ABC News.

The explosion leveled Waldrop's Gift Shop, the Tiger Lily Bookstore, Crest 5 & 10 Store owned by Mr. Berman, and of course, the Kopper Kettle.

From the time I was a goofy ten-year-old till I was a happy-go-lucky teenager, the Kopper Kettle nestled on the corner of Magnolia Avenue and Gay Street was the place to go for fast food in the heart of Auburn. Inside the glass walls, customers settled on round padded stools that hugged a coffee-stained counter. Behind the bar, cooks flipped 10-cent kettleburgers. But the thing I always ordered was a 15-cent slab of creamy coconut custard pie with crust as flaky as an ancient scroll. The baker wouldn't tell his secret, but when I dream of the smooth, airy filling I'd put my money on whipped egg whites, just the right amount of sugar and a subtle jolt of mace.

As a college student I made some midnight runs to the Kettle for strong, black coffee, Java potent enough to keep my eyes open to cram for this or that exam.

Later, after Jack's Hamburgers opened up across from the Auburn University Library on College Street, other burger joints became part of the bailiwick. But the Kopper Kettle was still the local meeting place where folks gathered to discuss everything from "crip" courses to politics, house parties to Vietnam, last night's date to tomorrow's dreams.

Students staggered in fighting sleep in the wee-hours. On dark moonless nights there was that light beaming on the corner inviting night owls to a safe, somewhat clean place to hang out. And older residents met at half past sun-up to solve the world's problems as they scarfed down two eggs, grits, toast slathered in butter and grape jelly, and as much high-octane coffee as they could hold – all for about 89-cents.

I moved away for a number of years but when I came back in the mid-seventies, the Kettle was still going strong. I didn't eat there as often as I had in earlier days, but I mourned the death of the Kopper Kettle as the end of an era.

Bad as it was, everybody knew it could have been so much worse. If it had happened a few minutes later, it would have been a disaster. But because it was a sleepy Sunday morning nobody was around when the blast went off.

The first folks to arrive on the scene were shocked when they saw lifeless bodies lying in the street. The explosion had jarred mannequins from the window of Parker's Department Store, which was where Behind the Glass is now. Stunned observers thought the dummies were real people.

As it turned out, no one was killed or injured in the explosion. Sad to say most of the adjoining buildings had to be demolished because structural damage from the blast made them unsafe. A local attorney, as well as a doctor and dentist with offices above the Kopper Kettle lost their records. One witness recalls that it was "raining flaming dental records." Some of these files were found 30 miles away. The Methodist church catty-cornered to the Kettle had the stained glass windows dating to 1873 blown out. The priceless pieces of glass were carefully placed in boxes and restored in Birmingham.

Over the years the Kopper Kettle faithful have met to deliver their eulogies to the diner. And long-time Auburn residents ask not "Where were you the day Kennedy was shot?" They ask instead, "Where were you when the Kettle blew up?"

Acknowledgments

The individual essays in *Second Cup* originally appeared in my weekly newspaper column. I am grateful to the publishers of the *Opelika-Auburn News* for permission to reprint these sketches in book form.

I thank my daughter Emily who helped me put this book together. She cheerfully assisted me as I chose which columns to use, and she managed the things that I didn't know how to do, such as getting it all on a thumb drive.

I am also grateful for daily encouragement from Mary Beth, my daughter who thinks I'm smarter, funnier, and kinder than I really am.

Many thanks to Tina Tatum of Solomon & George Publishers for giving me the opportunity to put *Second Cup* into print.

I greatly appreciate John Crenshaw's creative talents in designing the cover.

And a huge thank you to friends, acquaintances, and strangers who told me, "You need to put your columns in a book."

About the Author

Mary Adams Belk lives in Auburn, Alabama where her column appears weekly in the *Opelika-Auburn News*. She has published a number of short stories and nonfiction articles over the years. Her short stories have earned awards in several contests, including the Alabama Writers' Conclave competition. In another life, she spent almost two decades teaching anthropology at Auburn University. Because of her love of anthropology and writing, she combines the two whenever possible, weaving her anthropological background together with growing up in a small Southern college town to create stories that take an authentic look at people and places. When she isn't writing, she loves to travel with her daughter's Special Olympics gymnastics team, ride horses, hike, read, and go on archaeological digs.